I0820539

SHROOM

DISCLAIMER: Some mushrooms can be deadly, poisonous or cause illness, do not consume wild mushrooms.

First published in 2026 by OH
An Imprint of HEADLINE PUBLISHING GROUP LIMITED

1

Cataloguing in Publication Data is available from the British Library

ISBN 978-1-03543-408-4

Printed and bound in China by C&C Offset Printing Co., Ltd.

Headline's policy is to use papers that are natural, renewable and recyclable products and made from wood grown in well-managed forests and other controlled sources. The logging and manufacturing processes are expected to conform to the environmental regulations of the country of origin.

HEADLINE PUBLISHING GROUP LIMITED
An Hachette UK Company
Carmelite House
50 Victoria Embankment
London EC4Y 0DZ

The authorised representative in the EEA is Hachette Ireland, 8 Castlecourt Centre, Dublin 15, D15 XTP3, Ireland (email: info@hbgi.ie)

www.headline.co.uk
www.hachette.co.uk

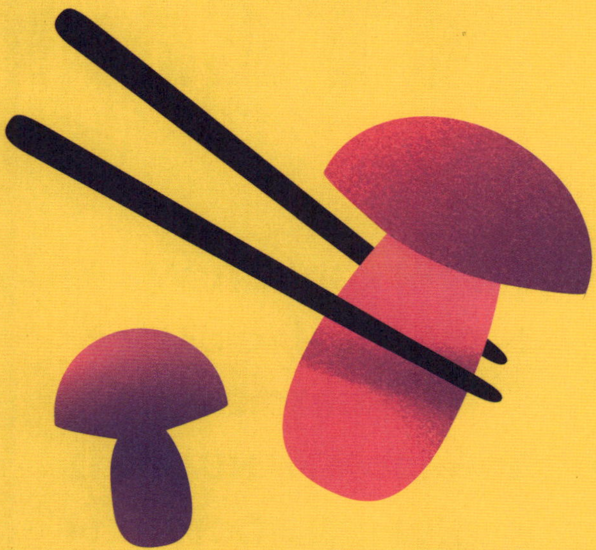

SHROOM

60 Umami-Packed Mushroom Recipes

EVIE HARBURY

CONTENTS

INTRODUCTION

I am, quite frankly, enamoured with, and fascinated by, 'shrooms'. In recent years, having spent a little more time observing mushrooms in food and exploring them, I have realized it's quite tricky not to become totally obsessed. I suppose you might be here because you're a fungi fan too. Let me tell you that this is a safe space for you. So, buckle up, grab your spatula and come along for the ride.

Mushrooms are often considered a superfood, and it's hard to argue otherwise. In addition to being a delicious mouthful, they can improve focus, energy and immunity. Packed full of nutrition, rich in vitamins and minerals, soaked in and from the soil and earth with no middle man (plant/stem/leaves), they are quite literally the most direct way of getting nutrients from the ground – a vessel that carries the nutrients from the rich forest floor to our digestive system. They contain powerful antioxidants and some are even known to contain probiotics that support a healthy gut microbiome. High in fibre and low in fat, they are also a great source of protein and B vitamins. Thank you, Earth, Mother Nature, for cultivating something so good for us and making it so tasty.

This book is a celebration of shrooms in the form of a collection of fun recipes for everyday life – bold, simple and packed full of flavour. There may be a stereotype that mushrooms are just the vegetarian option on a menu, or that every mushroom dish is destined to end up in the same dull brown and beige state, but I am excited to show you that this is simply not the case. These recipes celebrate the not-so-quiet brilliance of mushrooms.

The versatility of the shroom knows no bounds. They vary enormously in texture, from a chewy king oyster to the more delicate chanterelle, and can be incorporated into any part of a meal, including drinks and desserts!

Let's talk about understanding umami. Since you appreciate the flavour of mushrooms, you're halfway there. Umami is the fifth taste – alongside salty, sweet, bitter and sour. It is a deep savoury flavour that you can identify in Marmite, blue cheese and in mushrooms. It's the food version of a tannin that makes you smack your tongue against the roof of your mouth and want another bite. I like to think of umami as the taste that makes you come back wanting more.

Umami is apparent in all mushrooms, but is stronger in some than others. For example, porcini and shiitake (especially when dried) give the biggest umami boost to a plate, whereas chestnut and button shrooms offer a more subtle umami hit, which is exaggerated when pan-frying or grilling.

Mushrooms are a great accompaniment. They sit beautifully on a plate of full English breakfast, grilled alongside a steak and even complement a sophisticated fish dish. But they don't need to. They also stand on their own two feet.

Do mushrooms justice and make the dishes all about them! They deserve to be stars of the show and they truly have the bravado to carry a meal. Whether pride of place or on the side, mushrooms are a

flavour maker. They enrich any table of food they grace with their presence.

Antonio Carluccio, in his book *A Passion For Mushrooms*, said, 'There is nothing like a mushroom to fire the culinary imagination.' He's right! When thinking about dishes to put mushrooms into, I find myself rather undecided as to which of the endless possibilities of dishes to cook, as opposed to scratching my head and being at a loss for where to go.

Over the following pages, I would like to introduce mushrooms into places you may not have seen them before, but I assure you they fit in comfortably – such as tikka masala (page 78) or tacos (page 52).

But we also cannot shy away from the fact that there's a reason mushrooms are often paired with cheese, garlic and butter, and this is simply because these flavours enhance the earthy, umami flavours of which we are so fond. This gives us the age-old classics of vol-au-vents (page 26), mushroom stroganoff (page 104) and a host of delicious mushroom pasta dishes.

Through every recipe in this book, I keep to one unwavering principle, popularized by Shirley Conran in her 1975 book *Superwoman*: life is simply too short to stuff a mushroom!

MUSHROOMS ARE MAGICAL

Mushrooms are amazing in their otherworldliness – yet they are one of the most wholesome worldly things possible.

The more I've delved into my mushroom infatuation, the more I have realized how many ears prick up when you mention mushrooms – I often get the response, 'Oh I LOVE mushrooms!' There's that sparkle glimmering in someone's eye when you bring up a chanterelle, the lips puckering when you utter the word 'shiitake'. There must be something deep in the human mind that makes many of us find a mushroom as intriguing and addictive as we do. An unstoppable urge to look and admire, like when we spot a puppy, fumbling about on its wobbly legs. Something draws us to them.

The speed at which a mushroom grows is simply magic. They seem to pop up out of nowhere with no advance warning. I remember as a child seeing the freshly mowed lawn of our garden, and the next day, a field mushroom had sprouted, a good couple of inches higher than the grass. How quickly they appear in their strange forms with a shape unlike any other growing thing.

The forest floor, dappled with light, scattered with mushrooms, is an enchanted place. There's a reason mushrooms and toadstools appear in many a fairytale, because of the delightful feeling that surrounds them. The look of a mushroom is so whimsical that it begins to write the story by itself – no wonder they feature so prominently in storytelling and folklore. The way they sit proudly among the fallen trees, mossy patches and piles of pine needles only heightens their mythical qualities. New and exciting life springing from the most unlikely settings. Stumbling upon a perfect specimen of a mushroom springing from the pine needles, it is almost as if it is made of porcelain.

The shape of fungi is iconic and immediately recognizable. Even those without a penchant for eating mushrooms might be known to be obsessed with their silhouette. And, because of its intrigue, it is used as a motif in many a man-made item ... from cushions to coffee cups.

I look around my house, acknowledging somewhat that I am a mushroom enthusiast of sorts, and I notice mushroom depictions everywhere ... on my bathroom wallpaper, in a framed illustration in my hall, on the front cover of several books on my bookshelf (and not only cookbooks but other non-fiction and fiction alike), and a giant Yayoi Kusama poster with psychedelic-looking mushroom figures halfway up my stairs. This is paraphernalia that I have been drawn to and collected over the years but not intentionally or even consciously.

My grandma used to make me a wonderful mushroom-themed birthday dessert – a large rectangular tray of bright lime-green jelly that she would turn out onto a board and would then top with banana halves for mushroom stalks and meringues for the caps. The visual of this tray of food was so effective that I'd ask for it year after year – it dramatically surpassed the butterfly cupcakes and Barbie dress dome cake that came before it. Lime jelly, banana and meringue were perhaps not the most likely flavour combination, but the beauty of the mushroom motif far outweighed this.

The attraction of shrooms only makes them even more pleasing to put on your plate. Their parasols are so enjoyable to observe and their cross-sections are something I will never tire of. The gills, stalks and caps are so aesthetically agreeable. Nature is endlessly cool – leaves and flowers are wonderful things. But mushrooms – surely there's got to be some magic there (and no, not that kind!).

INGREDIENTS

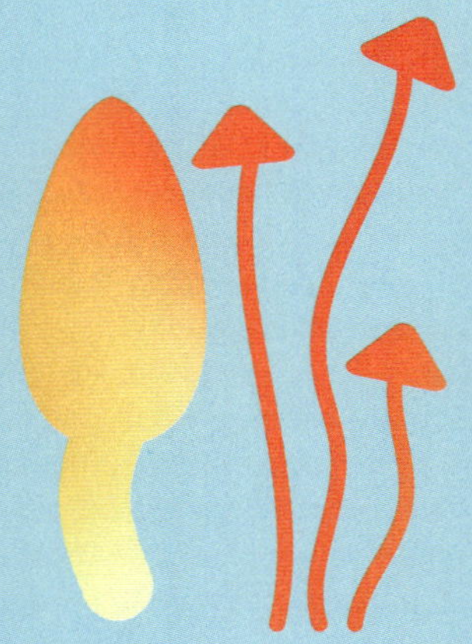

DRIED VS FRESH

Like many other cooks and chefs around the world, I can be guilty of being sceptical of a 'dried' ingredient. Dried herbs? Nope. Unless it's oregano, and I suppose in certain cases in Greek cuisine, mint, but apart from herbes de Provence, generally forget it. I have been known to turn my nose up at a stock cube in favour of the fresh liquid variety. Dried curry or bay leaves? Not interested. But this ends now – dried mushrooms are sometimes better than fresh. I use a mixture of dried and fresh mushrooms throughout my recipes. They cannot be used interchangeably as they give very different flavours and require different cooking techniques, but there is certainly a time and a place in the kitchen for dried mushrooms, and I'm going to tell you when.

Dried mushrooms tend to be punchier in their flavours and textures, whereas fresh ones can be more subtle. Where a rehydrated dried shiitake can be deliciously chewy, a fresh shiitake is soft and has little-to-no bite to it. Dried shiitake adds tons of deep, rich umami flavour to a dish, while fresh shiitake is great at absorbing other strong flavours such as teriyaki or miso.

And it's worth buying the highest quality dried mushrooms you can afford. In Hong Kong, I'm told this is the dried shiitake, identifiable by the cracks on its cap like a crackle-glazed pot straight out the kiln. With dried porcini, search for the slices where you can still make out the shape of the specimen, rather than finely chopped or broken pieces.

SUBSTITUTING MUSHROOMS

All of the dishes in this book have been written and developed with particular mushrooms in mind. That's not to say that you cannot use varieties interchangeably to a large extent, but it's worth noting that its texture rather than flavour that has usually determined the way a mushroom is cooked. For example, enoki have such a distinct, almost crunchy texture when served in their bundles that they are not so fit for braising and may be wasted by finely chopping them.

VEGETARIAN INGREDIENTS

To keep the recipes all vegetarian friendly, I have used vegetarian alternatives for fish sauce, Worcestershire sauce and oyster sauce. If you are feeding meat eaters, please feel free to use the non-vegetarian versions, and even chicken stock when vegetable stock is called for. Mushrooms are a brilliant (and very planet-friendly) alternative to meat in so many ways, with their incredible nutritional aspects and knockout flavour, so you do not need meaty flavours to accompany them. However, if you already have the original versions of the products listed above, they will work just perfectly.

EGGS

All eggs used in the recipes are large (US extra-large) and free-range.

BUTTER

Always unsalted, unless specified otherwise.

CHEESE

I have included only vegetarian cheeses in the ingredient lists, as many cheeses contain rennet, which is an animal product. However, the replacements that you could use interchangeably, if not feeding a vegetarian, are as follows:

Pecorino (v) to Parmesan
Dolcelatte (v) to Gorgonzola
Emmental (v) to Comte
Cornish Brie (v) to Taleggio or Camembert

HERBS

Mushrooms and herbs are great friends. In her book *The Flavour Thesaurus*, Niki Segnit observes that 'mushrooms feel at home with grassy herbs such as tarragon and parsley, but the woody herbs are their true kindred spirits'. You will notice I feature examples of both green herbs (such as chives, coriander/cilantro, parsley and tarragon) or woody herbs (such as thyme, rosemary and sage) in almost every recipe – these should always be fresh, not dried. The only exception would be the dried oregano that you'll find in the recipes for Meatless meatballs (page 64) and Portobello mushroom moussaka (page 108).

SALT

As they do with any food, salty ingredients enhance the flavour of mushrooms. This is why mushrooms go so well with hard cheese, soy sauce, fish sauce, pickles, olives, nori, kombu and other seaweeds, since they are all sources of salt. When these salt makers are present in the ingredients list, know that you may not have to season the food additionally.

PEPPER

I favour freshly ground black pepper (from a peppermill) or sometimes finely ground white pepper. Go easy on the white pepper, though – a little goes a long way.

SUGAR

Use standard white or brown sugar unless otherwise specified.

OTHER INGREDIENTS AND OVEN TEMPERATURES

Most of the more unusual ingredients should be available from most large supermarkets, but if not, please try your local Asian grocery store. Finally, all oven temperatures are for fan ovens, so please adjust according to your oven if it is not fan-assisted.

THE MUSHROOM MANUAL

HOW TO CHOOSE A MUSHROOM

In the supermarket, mushrooms often come in packets. Always choose the packet with the least-visible condensation on the inside, as this can sometimes indicate the mushrooms have been in and out of the refrigerator or that they might be getting a bit soggy or slimy. If they are loose, choose the smoother-looking, firmer mushrooms; if they have become dry and wrinkled, they are less fresh and may lack oomph, and they won't last very long in your refrigerator. If they have been sweating inside a packet, they may have a lingering dampness in their taste. When buying wild mushrooms, look for ones that are a little cleaner – if they are covered in dirt or forest debris, the likelihood is they might have some unwelcome tenants hunkering down in their caps. You will always have to clean some dirt off, but less is more.

HOW TO STORE A MUSHROOM

Remove it from any sweaty plastic packaging. Mushrooms are best kept in a brown paper bag, or in a bowl lined and loosely covered with paper towel. Like all fresh fruit or vegetables, fresh mushrooms deteriorate over time. Wild ones, especially, will be best in the first few days. Cultivated mushrooms will last 5–10 days if properly stored. Trust your nose – it can work out whether a mushroom is still good to eat. If it begins to smell damp, or even fishy, I'd argue that those are the flavours it'll bring to your dish and are best avoided. A good mushroom smells earthy, subtle and sometimes nutty.

HOW TO CLEAN A MUSHROOM

Mushrooms should always be cleaned of dirt before cooking. How often have you read, 'Clean your mushrooms ... but not with water' and been left feeling like a mushroom (kept in the dark!)? I'm here to tell you that 'cleaning' mushrooms does not refer to washing them, but to brushing them. You can do this very easily with a dry pastry brush or specialist 'mushroom brush' (or even an old toothbrush!) to remove any dirt from the caps and gills. If the stalk has stubborn dirt from where it met the earth, you can trim this off. It's best not to wash your mushrooms in water, as they are very quick to absorb any moisture, and mud, dirt or debris is much easier to brush off a dry mushroom. Especially important: do not get them wet if you're not planning to cook with them straight away, as they will go damp and soggy in the refrigerator. Sometimes a damp paper towel helps with the cleaning, but only if you're not having much luck with a brush.

The only exception to the 'do not wash' rule is for morels, which should be thoroughly dunked and shaken about in a bowl of cold water, briefly, just before cooking, to encourage any insects to get lost! Once washed, shake in a colander and then pat the mushrooms dry before cooking.

Maggots sometimes like wild mushrooms, and quite honestly, who can blame them? If you've got a punnet of particularly muddy or mossy wild mushrooms, give them a once-over for any uninvited dinner guests while you brush them clean.

HOW TO PREPARE A FRESH MUSHROOM

How to prepare your mushrooms largely depends on how you will cook them – or not cook them, as the case may be. There are a plenty of occasions where I enjoy a raw chestnut or button mushroom (such as in the mushroom skewers recipe on page 29 and bistro salad on page 118), where the freshest mushrooms you can find, well cleaned, are best. In these cases, chopping or slicing should be left to the last minute, just before serving. If cooking mushrooms, only on a few occasions would I encourage you to leave a chestnut or button mushroom whole – this has a time and a place, but I believe they are a completely different beast when chopped or sliced. Finely sliced mushrooms are my favourite. I think the texture is best of all, and they make for a hugely appetizing plate of food. Finely chopped mushrooms are perfect when using mushrooms as a stuffing or filling (such as in the gyoza recipe on page 36).

I remember a time when mushroom stalks were routinely removed before cooking – a satisfying task that was achieved by pressing the stalk to the side with your thumb, causing it to pop off – but I cannot see a reason for this other than if you want the mushroom sitting flat on the plate. If you do not love the very slightly firmer texture of a mushroom stalk, don't let it go to waste. Add it to a stock pot to add depth to your vegetable, chicken or beef stocks.

Halving or slicing mushrooms generally makes for the most visually pleasing presentation, showcasing the magnificent cross-sections we are so fond of. The texture of oyster and king oyster mushrooms, however, allows you to tear and shred them with your hands, which makes for a rougher surface than slicing that absorbs flavour well.

HOW TO COOK A MUSHROOM

Well, to put it simply, I am about to spend the rest of the book focusing on this, but let me run through the basics: mushrooms can be pickled, sautéed, deep-fried, boiled, baked, grilled, barbecued and more. In doing so, they usually shrink in size because of their high water content – not in as extreme a way as spinach, but the volume that you start with may halve by the time you are done cooking. The particularly big shrinkers are chestnut, hen of the woods and button mushrooms. Others appear to shrink as they soften, such as black trumpet, chanterelle and morel. So even if the quantity looks enormous to begin with, stick with me. If sautéing, grilling or pan-frying, the golden caramelization that the oil or butter gives the cooked mushroom adds a beautiful depth of umami flavour that I can only encourage.

HOW TO REHYDRATE A MUSHROOM

Place your dried mushrooms in a large heatproof bowl and pour boiling water over the top to generously cover, and leave for at least 30 minutes (large whole shiitake may take 1 hour) and up to overnight. The mushrooms will absorb all the water (so make sure you give them plenty) and grow, sometimes doubling in size. Wood ear mushrooms can expand up to four times their dried size, once rehydrated – much like those magic growing colourful dinosaur or alligator toys in the 1980s and 90s. Unlike the alligators, once the mushroom is rehydrated, you can gently squeeze out excess water, then finely chop or leave whole and use in the recipe as instructed.

MEETING THE MUSHROOMS

'Mushroom' is a broad term, so let's get more technical for a moment. In addition to the different mushroom names you'll find in the hundreds of languages around the world, we also have different names for mushroom varieties in English. So, to avoid confusion, I want to briefly outline these names and give you a quick run-down of the different mushrooms that appear in the recipes in this book. Each variety also has a Latin name, which I won't go into, but there are plenty of books that do, if you're interested. The visual diversity of all these mushrooms is astounding. Not only are they not all just brown and beige, but the shapes and forms they take make each one unique.

BLACK TRUMPET – also **trompette de la mort** or **horn of plenty** – as the name suggests, a deep black mushroom that looks like it shouldn't be edible, but it is, and it's delicious! Contrary to the 'de la mort' the French name suggests, these are not a mushroom of death but of flavour. The whimsical shape of the horn of plenty looks as though it has almost been formed out of tissue paper.

BUTTON (7) – also known as **white** mushroom – a mild, subtle-flavoured mushroom that keeps its shape. One of the most common mushrooms worldwide. Great for sautéing for sauces. A beautiful vessel for flavour.

CHANTARELLE, girolle or **golden chantarelle (4)** – a bright egg-yolk yellow wild mushroom with fruity notes. They have an apricot aroma and subtle taste, but are also quite peppery and savoury too. These are golden gems of the forest floor and an absolute treat to cook with and eat.

CHESTNUT (6) – also known as **cremini** and **brown** mushroom (can also come in a button variety) – is the most common mushroom in British and North American cooking. It is cultivated all around the world, which also makes it the most readily available and the cheapest of the shrooms. Very versatile in its cooking and its flavour pairings. If they are all you can get hold of, they can be pretty much used anywhere a fresh mushroom is required.

ENOKI (3) – rarely, but sometimes known as **enokitake** – sold in bunches of loads of little white mushrooms grown in a cluster. They are decidedly otherworldly looking, especially once deep-fried (Crispy enoki, page 30). Enoki are popular in Chinese, Japanese and Korean cooking and are now fairly readily available all over the world, if sometimes a little pricey.

HEN OF THE WOODS or **maitake (11)** – an incredible mushroom with a full-on flavour. It is sold in its clusters, where I think it should stay to be cooked. Pressed down in a pan or deep-fried, it crisps up beautifully and takes on marinades wonderfully.

KING OYSTER (5) – despite the name being the same as the regular 'oyster' mushroom opposite, these are a very different proposition, both in look and texture. The king oyster is all stalk, no talk. The flesh holds its shape, and the firmness that it retains through the cooking process is unique. Shredding in a distinctive, pulled pork-esque way, this mushroom is often cooked as a meat replacement because of its look and ability to take on any spices thrown its way.

LION'S MANE, bearded tooth or **pom pom mushroom** – available in powdered form and mostly known for its superpower qualities. In a coffee or another hot drink, or even in a dessert, this mushroom has so many features that you will want to add it to your daily routine, I'm sure of it. More on this in chapter 6.

MOREL (1) – with the look of a dark brown loose-knit woolly hat fit for a fairy. If you came across this mushroom for the first time, you may second-guess whether it was edible. However, not only are they edible, but they are an absolute delight to cook with and munch on. Their taste is deep and smoky – and they are high on any chef's cook list. Cleaning requires a smidge of patience, with all the nooks and crannies, but nothing worth having comes easy. Take one bite of a pan-fried morel and let it do the talking.

OYSTER (2) – easily cultivated and even available to be grown at home with 'grow-your-own' mushroom kits. Oyster mushrooms grow in clusters, and they come in all manner of pastel colours – yellow, grey and even pink. These are a subtly aromatic mushroom, with a meaty texture, especially when grilled.

PORCINI – also known as **cep/cèpe**, **bolete**, **penny bun** and **king bolete** – only ever found in the wild, as we haven't quite figured out the maze of complex requirements to cultivate this one. It is usually bought dried, because it requires specific growing conditions and has such a short season. When rehydrated, the soaking liquor is deliciously rich and deep brown. You can add this to your cooking as a mushroom stock of sorts, but keep in mind that it may overtake some of the more subtle flavours in a dish. There are, in fact, many types of porcini, but for the purposes of the recipes included and in the interest of keeping this book light, I've grouped them together.

PORTOBELLO – these big boys are the same variety as a chestnut mushroom, but more mature. In the 1980s and 90s they were often stuffed and breadcrumbed. Now they are regularly found as the vegetarian option on a barbecue. They work well in slices and hold their shape. They have dark, inky gills that hold a depth of shroomy flavour.

SHIITAKE (9) – made popular by Chinese and Japanese cuisines and now a common ingredient worldwide. They can be cultivated, which brings their price down compared to other wild mushroom varieties and are just as often sold both fresh and dried. They keep their shape perfectly when cooked and retain a chewy and moist texture.

SHIMEJI (8,10) – also known as **beech** mushrooms – often found with both brown and white caps. They have nutty qualities, in both taste and look. They look bonkers in their clusters, in an appealing sort of way. Their mild nutty smell lends itself to being paired with nuts. The walnut miso paste of the udon bowl on page 74 makes the shimeji taste even nuttier.

WOOD EAR or **black fungus** – a Chinese and Cantonese staple. Available dried, they are rehydrated for cooking. Sometimes they are already sliced or shredded in their packaging. They are very delicately flavoured but once rehydrated, add a particularly interesting texture to a dish.

(See reference image overleaf)

1
2
3
4
5
6

7
8
9
10
11

MUSHROOMS OF THE WORLD

Yet another exciting thing about mushrooms is just how many countries have them in common as an ingredient. All over the world, cultures have figured out something great to do with mushrooms. Pretty much every continent uses them as a staple or at least a feature in all manner of cuisines. The magic of mushrooms is how they can slot in, find a home and improve so many dishes.

Many countries have a favourite mushroom. In the eyes of many Italians, the porcini mushroom is a good reason to look forward to autumn, while they pretty much ignore all other shrooms. In his book *Close Encounters of the Fungal Kind*, Richard Fortey describes porcini as 'simultaneously delicate and forthright', and says that 'it is understandable that so many Italians are obsessed by porcini'. There is, in fact, an entire annual festival devoted to the porcini mushroom, where they worship its existence, in the town of Borgo Val di Taro.

In France, the chanterelle takes centre stage. It doesn't work so well as a dried mushroom, so in its season from the end of summer to mid-winter, it is celebrated by being cooked in all manner of ways – be it sautéed in butter, or folded into eggs or cream sauces. They are often treated gently, allowing their delicate flavour to be celebrated – nothing too bold is added to overshadow the chanterelle.

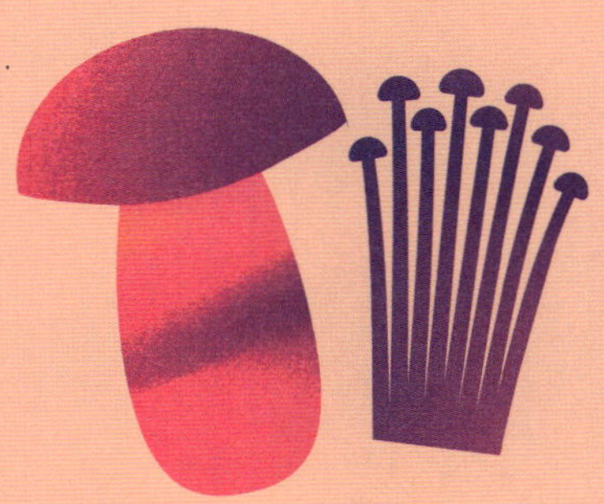

In England, it would be the modest chestnut mushroom, with its appearance on many a plate throughout the day; from its important role in a full English breakfast to accompanying a steak at dinner.

In Japanese cuisine, shiitake both fresh and dried are enjoyed in dishes from ramen to bento from udon to soba, and sometimes might as well be the only mushroom available. In Chinese cuisine, although dried shiitake features quite often, the wood ear makes a very frequent appearance in salads, stir-fries and in spring roll and dumpling fillings.

Europeans are the world's leading lovers of wild mushrooms. Particularly Eastern Europe, where the abundant forest floors are scattered with fungi, and the pastime of mushrooming is an inherited gift through the generations.

An increase in mushroom hunting in England and the USA over the last century is likely to have coincided with the increase in Europeans moving abroad. With more Czechs chasing the chanterelle and Italians in pursuit of porcinis, mushrooming has become an evermore popular activity.

Over the recipes in this book, I'd like to take a whistle-stop tour around the world in mushrooms and explore flavours from different cuisines. Sometimes this will be where mushrooms are commonly found – in pasta, stroganoff or ramen-style dishes – sometimes where they can comfortably be inserted, such as jerk or moussaka recipes, and sometimes where you wouldn't expect to find them at all, such as in a martini or tiramisu!

TALK SEASONS TO ME

Wild mushrooms are very seasonal so, unsurprisingly, you'll find they will be most expensive when they are not naturally in season. Most of the recipes that use chanterelle, black trumpet and morels can be made with other wild mushrooms that are cheaper or available at that time or year. The cooking of each mushroom may vary slightly (cook chanterelles for less time and hen of the woods for longer, for example), but the recipe can be just as delicious.

Mushrooming is a wonderful hobby but you have to know what you are doing. It taps into our natural human instinct to gather food ourselves. My advice is to learn from a professional – never try by yourself. Go out mushroom hunting with an expert guide, where you can learn and consult the expert before going home and devouring your findings. Many wild mushrooms can be poisonous, and it's not worth the risk if you are unsure.

I prefer to do my mushroom hunting at markets and there's no shame in you doing the same! As a market shopper, I still notice the seasonality of mushrooms. The main mushroom season in Europe begins in late summer and carries through to the early/mid-winter. Fresh mushrooms give autumnal vibes, and quite rightly, because this is when they are most in season.

Chanterelles have a winter variety, which grows after the season of the yellow chanterelle, and these are more delicate, with yellow stems but small brown caps. Just as delicious, they can be used as a substitute for whenever you would have used the bright yellow chanterelle version.

Morels have a particularly short growing season in spring; they are only available for about a month, but you can buy them dry and rehydrate them to cook as you would fresh.

Seasonality is less of an issue with cultivated mushrooms as the cultivated shroom of the supermarket shelf is a different beast. Not insignificant, not worthless, just different and widely available all year round. Because of this availability and the ability to be grown to meet demand, they are significantly cheaper. Cultivated mushrooms are grown in sheds or warehouses that imitate caves, in carefully controlled dimmed light, and although they lack the welcome mustiness of a woodland floor, they still offer tasty umami properties. Officially, there is no hierarchy. Unofficially, wild ones are more coveted, and the price tag reflects this.

HOW TO USE THIS BOOK

By trying out the recipes in this book, I hope you will learn plenty of different ways to cook mushrooms and will adapt recipes you know and love to make mushroom versions of them too. Rather than squeezing mushrooms in where they don't belong, I hope you will see this as an opportunity to explore their versatility.

If you are using this book as an introduction to cooking with (and eating) mushrooms, I suggest you start with something that you already know, for example the pizza on page 98 or gyoza on page 36, and try these mushroom versions. If you're here looking for a place to get more experimental with your mushrooming, make it happen with a biriyani (page 76) or tempura (page 24).

If you're not sure what style of dish you are in the mood for, be guided, steered and led by what you have in your fridge (or in your forest). Use the index to search the recipes by mushroom type.

The best recipes are the ones you return to, the ones that, once you've cooked them the first time, you can read between the detailed instructions and improvise if you need to. Once you realize that you can add other ingredients in or remove something that you do not like, the recipe really becomes your own.

VEGAN FRIENDLY

If you are looking for a quick route to the vegan recipes in the book, there are plenty, and they are as follows:

Oyster mushroom satay (page 34)
Shiitake gyoza (page 36)
Jerk-style hen of the woods (page 49)
Shredded king oyster tacos (page 52)
Shiitake onigiri bento box (page 54)
Mushroom larb in lettuce cups (page 60)
Thai green curry (page 72)
Miso and walnut udon noodle bowl (page 74)
Wood ear Vietnamese spring rolls (page 80)
Tom yum soup (page 86)
Shiitake yaki soba (page 88)
Mushroom and chickpea rendang (page 92)
Smacked cucumber and wood ear mushroom salad (page 130)
Sticky shiitake and shimeji rice (page 132)
Ginger stir-fried mushroom and pak choi (page 138)
Dirty mushroom martini (page 144)
Lion's mane iced coconut latte (page 146)

There are also plenty of other recipes that can be made vegan very easily, by substituting plant-based butters, mayonnaise, yoghurts, honey, milks and creams.

DIFFICULTY

Each recipe has been assigned a difficulty rating, as follows:

Easy: this recipe requires no complex skills and is quick to make.

Medium: this recipe may need a bit more focus, but it'll be worth it.

Difficult: this could be the perfect recipe for when you are wanting to learn a new kitchen skill, or to spend a little more time in the kitchen to impress your guests.

Even the most difficult recipes that lie ahead will still be totally achievable for the home cook, and use regular kitchen equipment. I would like to encourage you to see the difficulty level as an exciting challenge, and not let it put you off. It is there for a time indication as much as anything – I believe that all these recipes are within your reach, and a little challenge is good for the soul! I also recognize that sometimes one is in desperate need of a quick, easy shroom fix!

BITES TO BEGIN

What better bite to begin than a brilliantly bold mushroom? These mini but mighty dishes are great mushroom nibbles to start a meal. Finger foods for the fungi-obsessed ... featuring skewers, toasts and canapés. You could build a whole meal out of these if you wanted to keep things snacky.

King oyster, shiitake and vegetable tempura

SERVES 4 AS A STARTER OR SIDE

DIFFICULTY 🍄🍄

DIPPING SAUCE

100 ml (3½ fl oz) boiling water
1 dried shiitake mushroom
1 piece kombu, optional
1 tbsp caster (superfine) sugar
2 tbsps soy sauce
1 tbsp mirin
1 tbsp sake

TEMPURA

125 g (4 oz) self-raising (self-rising) flour
pinch of fine salt
pinch of white pepper
225 ml (8 fl oz) ice-cold sparkling water
1 egg
100 g (3½ oz) king oyster mushrooms, sliced
50 g (2 oz) shiitake mushrooms, whole and scored
100 g (3½ oz) sweet potato, peeled and cut into ½ cm (¼ in) slices
½ white onion, sliced
50 g (2 oz) tenderstem broccoli
8 shiso leaves, optional
vegetable oil, for deep-frying

You can tempura any mushrooms you like, and any vegetables such as fennel, aubergine (eggplant), pumpkin or green beans. Kombu (used here in the dipping sauce) is a type of dried edible seaweed, common in Japanese cooking. It adds a huge depth of flavour to sauces that are flavoured with dried mushrooms. You could include these as part of the bento box on page 54.

1. For the dipping sauce, pour the boiling water over the dried shiitake and kombu in a heatproof bowl or jug. Leave to steep for at least 10 minutes, then stir in the sugar, soy sauce, mirin and sake. Remove the mushroom and kombu to serve. You can keep this sauce in the refrigerator if you'd prefer to serve cold.
2. Fill a large heavy-bottomed saucepan with the oil to about halfway, and heat until about 180°C (350°F). Line a baking tray with paper towel.
3. For the tempura batter, stir together the flour, salt and white pepper in a large bowl. Gradually pour in the sparkling water, whisking as you go, and then whisk in the egg, until you have a smooth batter.
4. Dip your prepared mushrooms and other veg into the batter and then carefully use tongs to place straight into the hot oil. Leave to cook for 2–3 minutes, until lightly browned and crispy, turning halfway through. Remove with tongs and place on the paper towel-lined baking tray to drain any excess oil.
5. Plate up to serve warm straight away, with the dipping sauce on the side.

Vol-au-vents

MAKES 14

DIFFICULTY

1 x 320 g (11 oz) sheet of puff pastry
1 egg yolk
15 g (½ oz) butter
1 shallot, finely diced
1 garlic clove, chopped
150 g (5 oz) button mushrooms, finely sliced
100 ml (3½ fl oz) double (heavy) cream
small bunch of parsley (or tarragon), chopped, plus extra to serve
½ tsp lemon juice
sea salt flakes and freshly ground black pepper

These are a bit of a retro canapé - so let's travel back to the 1970s and take a delicious bite of nostalgia. The pastry cases can be baked up to five days in advance and kept in a sealed container at room temperature once cool.

1. Preheat the oven to 180°C fan (350°F).
2. Use a 5 cm (2 in) round or fluted cutter to cut out 28 circles of puff pastry. Use a 3.5 cm (1.5 in) cutter to cut the middle out of 14 of the circles and discard the centre piece.
3. Brush the circles and rings with egg yolk and then place the rings on top of the circles and press down lightly. Transfer to a lined baking tray and cook for 12–14 minutes. Once cooked, carefully press down the middles to make room for the filling.
4. Meanwhile, heat the butter in a large frying pan (skillet) over a medium-high heat and fry the shallot for 2–3 minutes.
5. Add in the garlic and mushrooms, season generously with salt and pepper and cook for 6–8 minutes until the mushrooms have begun to caramelize.
6. Stir in the cream and mix through the mushrooms for 30 seconds, then remove from the heat and stir in the parsley and lemon juice.
7. Fill the cooked pastry cases with the mushroom mixture, scatter with parsley and serve immediately.

Top left: Miso mushroom bites (page 28)
Top right: Vol-au-vents (page 26)
Bottom: Raw chestnut mushroom skewers (page 29)

Miso mushroom bites

MAKES ABOUT 20

DIFFICULTY 🍄🍄

200 g (7 oz) king oyster mushrooms
1 tbsp vegetable oil
30 g (1 oz) red or brown miso
½ tbsp mirin
½ tbsp sugar
½ tbsp sake
pinch of white pepper
2 tsps rice vinegar
3 tbsps water
1 tsp soy sauce
15 g (½ oz) butter
1 tsp cornflour (cornstarch)
1 tsp toasted white sesame seeds, to serve

Glazed in a sweet miso marinade, these umami-packed mushroom bites could be served on cocktail sticks as a canapé. They also make a great side dish or you can serve over rice as a main. You can make them in advance and reheat to serve on a lined tray in a hot oven.

1. Cut the mushrooms in half, and then across into bitesize pieces, and score the flat side in a diamond pattern.
2. Pour the oil into a frying pan (skillet) and pan-fry the mushroom pieces, scored side down, over a medium-high heat, for 6–8 minutes, until golden. Flip over and fry for a further 5–6 minutes until golden and tender.
3. Meanwhile make the miso glaze. In a small saucepan, combine the miso, mirin, sugar, sake, pepper, vinegar, water, soy sauce, butter and cornflour. Stir over a gentle heat for 1–2 minutes until the butter has melted, then remove from the heat.
4. Turn the mushroom heat down to low, pour the glaze over the mushrooms and flip them to coat both sides. Cook for a further 1–2 minutes, until the mushrooms are glazed in the thick miso sauce.
5. Plate up and sprinkle with sesame seeds. Serve warm, with cocktail sticks.

Raw chestnut mushroom skewers

MAKES 20

DIFFICULTY

75 g (2½ oz) Gouda (or Emmental), at room temperature
5 baby chestnut mushrooms
5 pickled chillies (or 10 pickled cocktail onions)
20 pitted green olives

A perfect aperitif at cocktail hour to have alongside your Dirty mushroom martini (page 144) before dinner. Eating mushrooms raw seems to be more common in France than the rest of the world, but I'd like to normalize it. These skewers are a little inspired by a *gilda*, a Spanish tapas skewer that is typically made of olive, anchovy and pickled chilli. It's worth using good-quality olives (I like Perello) and pickles for this one.

1. Cut the cheese into 20 small cubes, the chestnut mushrooms into quarters and each chilli into 4 pieces.
2. On each cocktail stick thread one piece of cheese, one piece of chilli (or half a cocktail onion), one quarter of a mushroom and one olive.
3. Serve cold.

Crispy enoki
with creamy lemon dipping sauce

SERVES 4 AS A SNACK

DIFFICULTY 🍄

25 g (1 oz) cornflour (cornstarch)
25 g (1 oz) plain (all-purpose) flour
½ tsp chilli powder
¼ tsp garlic granules
fine salt and white pepper
75 ml (2½ fl oz) ice-cold water
150 g (5 oz) enoki mushrooms
vegetable oil, for frying

DIP

2 tbsps mayonnaise (Kewpie, if you like)
1 tbsp sour cream
2 tsps freshly squeezed lemon juice
spring onion (scallion), sliced, to serve

These delicate enoki mushrooms are deep-fried in a light batter, making them deliciously snackable. Enoki are a lesser-known but very versatile mushroom. When deep-fried they explode into wacky shapes and go incredibly crispy.

1. Heat a saucepan half full of vegetable oil to 180°C (350°F).
2. Make the batter by stirring together the cornflour, flour, chilli powder, garlic granules, salt and pepper in a large bowl. Add the ice-cold water and whisk to get rid of any lumps.
3. Cut the enoki horizontally into thin slices about 1–2 mm (1/16 in) thick.
4. Dip each slab of enoki into the batter and then carefully place it into the oil to cook for 2 minutes, turning halfway through. Once cooked, remove from the oil and place on paper towels to remove excess oil.
5. Make the dip by stirring together the mayonnaise, sour cream and lemon juice.
6. Serve the enoki warm, with the dip on the side and spring onion scattered on top.

Grilled goat's cheese and mushroom toasts

MAKES 10–12

DIFFICULTY

1 red onion, sliced
1½ tbsps extra virgin olive oil
1 tsp red wine (or sherry) vinegar
1 tsp soft light brown sugar
100 g (3½ oz) mixed mushrooms, sliced
sea salt flakes and freshly ground black pepper
1 baguette, sliced
2–3 tomatoes, sliced
150 g (5 oz) rind-on goat's cheese, sliced

TO SERVE

balsamic glaze, optional
micro herbs (such as micro thyme, parsley or basil), optional

The tanginess of goat's cheese is a particularly reliable flavour combination with mushrooms. These toasts could be served as a canapé or a starter – they have enough substance to kickstart the meal without stealing the show.

1. Start by making the caramelized onion. Cook the onion in a teaspoon of oil in a medium frying pan (skillet) for 20 minutes over a low heat, stirring occasionally, until golden and soft.
2. Add the vinegar and sugar and cook for another 3 minutes, until jammy, then remove from the heat and set aside.
3. Heat the grill (broiler) to medium, about 220°C (430°F) if your oven gives you the choice.
4. Arrange the mushrooms on a baking tray, drizzle with the remaining oil and season with salt and pepper. Grill for 4–5 minutes.
5. Cut the baguette into 10–12 x 1 cm (½ in) slices. Arrange on a baking tray and lightly toast under the grill for 1 minute on each side.
6. Remove from the grill and spread each piece with some caramelized onion and place a slice of tomato on each. Top with a slice or two of goat's cheese and grill for 4–5 minutes.
7. When the cheese is bubbling, spoon some mushrooms on top.
8. Serve warm, finished with a drizzle of balsamic glaze, or a scattering of micro herbs if you like.

Oyster mushroom satay
with peanut sauce

MAKES 4 SKEWERS

DIFFICULTY 🍄🍄

1 tsp mild curry powder
½ tsp ground turmeric
2.5 cm (1 in) fresh ginger root, grated
zest and juice of ½ lime
2 tbsps coconut milk
1 tbsp vegetable oil
sea salt flakes
200 g (7 oz) oyster mushrooms

PEANUT SAUCE

3 tbsps crunchy peanut butter
½ tbsp soy sauce
1 tbsp agave or honey
juice of ½ lime

TO SERVE

lime wedges
cucumber, sliced
Thai shallots, sliced
peanuts, chopped (optional)

All the classic flavours of a typical satay skewer. Oyster mushrooms take to the coconut and curry spices like a duck to water. These are best enjoyed as a starter or side. A brilliant dish to serve to someone who is perhaps unsure about mushrooms to get them on board – the texture of the grilled oyster mushroom is surprisingly meaty.

1. Preheat the grill (broiler) to high.
2. In a small bowl combine the curry powder, turmeric, ginger, lime zest and juice, coconut milk, oil and a pinch of salt to make a satay marinade.
3. Skewer the mushrooms onto 4 long metal skewers (if you only have wooden ones, soak them in water for 1 hour before using). Place the skewers onto a foil-lined baking tray. Use a pastry brush to coat the mushrooms with the marinade on both sides.
4. Grill for 10–12 minutes, until charred, turning halfway through.
5. Meanwhile, add all the peanut sauce ingredients into a bowl and stir together until combined.
6. Serve the skewers warm, with the peanut sauce in a pot on the side topped with chopped peanuts, along with the sliced cucumber, shallots and lime wedges.

Shiitake gyoza

with ponzu dipping sauce

MAKES 16–20

DIFFICULTY

60 g (2 oz) shiitake mushrooms, finely chopped
50 g (2 oz) Chinese cabbage, finely chopped
50g (2 oz) daikon (mouli) or carrot, grated
2 garlic cloves, peeled and crushed
2 cm (½ inch) fresh ginger root, peeled and minced
1 spring onion (scallion), finely chopped
2 sprigs of coriander (cilantro), leaves and stalks, finely chopped
2 tsps sesame oil
2 tsps soy sauce
2 tsps mushroom oyster sauce
2 tsps cornflour (cornstarch), plus extra for dusting
pinch of pepper (preferably white pepper)
16–20 gyoza wrappers (depending on size)
1 tbsp vegetable oil
Japanese seven-spice, to garnish, optional

PONZU DIPPING SAUCE

1 tsp freshly squeezed lime juice
1½ tbsps soy sauce
1 tsp mirin
1 tsp rice vinegar
1 tbsp water

Gyoza are delicious little Japanese dumplings that have loads of different fillings neatly folded away inside. Using ready-made gyoza wrappers, they are far simpler to make than you might realize. If you don't have fresh shiitake, you can simply rehydrate dried ones by pouring boiling water over them and leaving to steep for 30 minutes.

1. For the gyoza filling, mix the prepped mushrooms, cabbage, daikon or carrot, garlic, ginger, spring onion and coriander together in a bowl and add the sesame oil, soy sauce, mushroom oyster sauce, cornflour and pepper. Stir until completely combined.
2. Prepare a small cup of water on your work surface. Hold a gyoza wrapper in the flat palm of your hand (or on the work surface) and place a teaspoon of the filling mixture into the middle of the wrapper. Dip your finger in the water and wet a ring around the edge of the wrapper. Fold one half of the wrapper up to meet the other, pinch a corner together, fold creases in the wrapper and pinch together to fully close. It does not matter too much how you do this so long as it is sealed. Repeat with all the mixture and wrappers and transfer them to a plate or tray dusted with cornflour.
3. For the dipping sauce, stir together all the ingredients in a small bowl and set aside.
4. Next, heat the vegetable oil in a lidded saucepan over a medium-low heat. Add in the dumplings in a single layer over the base of the saucepan. Prepare 3 tablespoons of water and have the lid ready. Pour the water into the pan and very quickly put the lid on. Leave to cook for 5–6 minutes then remove the gyoza from the pan.
5. Serve immediately with the dipping sauce in a pot on the side. Finish with Japanese seven spice, if you like.

Broad bean and wild mushroom dumplings

MAKES 20

DIFFICULTY

250 g (9 oz) 00 flour
pinch of fine salt
120 ml (4 fl oz) water
15 g (½ oz) butter
1 egg yolk
4 tbsps vegetable oil
1 onion, sliced
½ small onion, finely diced
150 g (5 oz) wild mushrooms (any), chopped
125 g (4 oz) broad beans (or peas)
50 g (2 oz) soft cheese (such as tvarog or cream cheese)
30 g (1 oz) salted butter
sea salt flakes and black pepper, to season

TO SERVE

200 g (7 oz) sour cream, to serve
chives, chopped, to serve

These beautiful little pillows are based on the Polish *pierogi*, where typically potato and *tvarog* (a curd cheese) are wrapped up in a soft dough, and then boiled and pan-fried.

1. To make the dough, place the flour in a large bowl and add salt. In a small saucepan add the water and butter and warm through. Once the butter has melted (but the water is not yet bubbling), pour this straight into the flour along with the egg yolk and stir with a wooden spoon to mix. When combined, transfer to a clean surface, knead for 5 minutes until smooth then cover with a damp tea towel and leave to rest at room temperature for about 30 minutes.
2. Pour the oil into a sauté pan over a high heat and add the sliced onion. Season with salt and reduce the heat to medium. Cook for 8–10 minutes until golden and crispy then drain in a sieve over a heatproof bowl.
3. Return the pan to the heat and add the diced onion, frying for 5–6 minutes until softened. Add in the mushrooms for 3–4 minutes then decant into a bowl and place in the fridge to cool. Add the broad beans to the empty pan and cook for 2–3 minutes. Next, place the broad beans, cheese and salt and pepper into a food processor and blitz until smooth. Add to the cooling mushroom mixture and return to the fridge.
4. Roll the dough out on a lightly floured surface until as thin as possible (about 1 mm) and cut out 9 cm (3.5 in) circles (with a cutter or the top of a glass). Place one tablespoon of filling into the middle of each of the circles and fold over into half-moons. Press the edges together ensuring the filling stays inside and press a fork down around the rounded edge to seal.
5. Bring a large pan of salted water to the boil. Once boiling, add the dumplings in batches and cook for 2–3 minutes, until they float to the top, then drain.
6. Melt the salted butter in a frying pan (skillet) over a medium heat. Add the dumplings to the butter and fry for 1–2 minutes on each side.
7. Serve the warm dumplings on a bed of sour cream and top with the fried onions and some chopped chives.

Barbecued enoki rolls and shiitake skewers

MAKES 6 SKEWERS

DIFFICULTY

1 tbsp vegetable oil
1 aubergine (eggplant), cut into ¼ cm (⅛ in) slices lengthways
80 g (3 oz) enoki, cut into 9 pieces – try to keep in bundles
9 shiitake mushrooms

MARINADE

3 tbsps dark soy sauce
2 tbsps honey (or caster/superfine sugar)
1 tbsp rice vinegar
½ tbsp Shaoxing wine
juice of 1 lime
1 tsp English mustard
2 garlic cloves
2.5 cm (1 in) fresh ginger root
1–2 red chillies
1 spring onion (scallion)
1 tbsp vegetable (or sesame) oil
small bunch of coriander (cilantro), leaves and stalks, finely chopped

Many Cantonese recipes that I cook in my daily life are inspired by my friend and colleague Jeremy Pang. Mushrooms feature heavily. This is my own take on a Hong Kong barbecue classic. Skewers such as these (but with the enoki wrapped in beef) might be cooked over coals, barbecues or even in a home kitchen all around Hong Kong. The aubergine wrap is my beef substitute. Serve as a snack or side, or even as a main on a bed of steamed jasmine rice.

1. Place 6 wooden skewers into water to soak for at least 1 hour, or overnight.
2. To make the marinade, blitz the soy sauce, honey, vinegar, wine, lime juice, mustard, garlic, ginger, chillies and spring onion together in a food processor until smooth. Stir in the oil and chopped coriander. Set aside.
3. For the enoki rolls, pour the oil into a frying pan (skillet) and heat. Add the aubergine slices and fry for 2 minutes on each side over a medium-high heat.
4. Wrap each bundle of enoki in 1 slice of cooked aubergine and thread onto the wooden skewers, 3 rolls per skewer.
5. Then thread the shiitake mushrooms onto the 3 remaining skewers, using 3 mushrooms per skewer.
6. Brush the marinade over both types of mushroom skewers and grill over a barbecue for 3–4 minutes on each side to cook through (or place under a hot grill/broiler for 8–10 minutes), brushing with more marinade throughout the cooking process.

SMALL PLATES FOR BIG MINDS

This section combines dishes that could be considered more appropriate for lunches than dinners. Food to eat at home or for a packed lunch. Similarly to Bites to Begin, these tasty small plates can be used in a sharing or tapas-style menu. They work brilliantly in a multitude of combinations when you want to showcase the range of dishes in your mushroom repertoire.

Portobello banh mi

MAKES 2 SANDWICHES

DIFFICULTY

PICKLE
1 tbsp sugar
1 tbsp boiling water
1 tbsp cider vinegar
40 g (1½ oz) carrot, peeled and sliced into matchsticks
40 g (1½ oz) daikon (mooli) or radish, sliced into matchsticks

MUSHROOM PATÉ
10 g (½ oz) butter
½ onion, chopped
1 star anise
150 g (5 oz) chestnut mushrooms, chopped
1 tsp soy sauce
½ tsp rice vinegar
pinch of white pepper

MUSHROOMS
1 tbsp vegetable oil
4 portobello mushrooms, sliced
2 tbsp cornflour (cornstarch)
1 tsp honey
juice of ½ lime
1 tsp vegan fish sauce
1 tsp soy sauce

TO SERVE
2 small baguettes (or 1 large cut in half)
sriracha
cucumber, sliced or ribboned
coriander (cilantro)
Thai basil
red chillies, sliced

This filling lunch is a mushroom take on the classic Vietnamese sandwich. It's a texture and taste explosion inside a crunchy fluffy baguette. The traditional banh mi baguette can be tricky to source, so a French stick is a good substitute. This is a total mixture of textures and flavours that perfectly complement each other. Refreshing pickles, aromatic herbs, crunchy cucumber and smooth paté - this sandwich has it all.

1. For the pickle, place the sugar in a heatproof jug or bowl and pour in the boiling water. Stir until dissolved then add the vinegar. Add the sliced carrot and daikon into the pickling liquid and set aside to pickle while you prepare the rest of the sandwich.
2. Make the paté by heating the butter over a medium heat in a frying pan (skillet). Add the onion and star anise and sweat for 3–4 minutes, then turn up the heat and add the mushrooms. Cook for another 5–6 minutes until the moisture has reduced and the mixture is caramelized. Remove from the heat and stir through the soy sauce, vinegar and pinch of pepper. Remove the star anise and transfer the mixture into a food processor to blend until smooth. Set aside to cool.
3. Add the oil into a frying pan and place over a high heat. Dust the portobello mushrooms in cornflour and place in the oil to cook for 7–8 minutes. Then add in the honey, lime juice, fish sauce and soy sauce and cook for 1 minute more before taking off the heat.
4. Halve the baguettes lengthways and scoop out the squishy middle of the bread and discard (or keep for breadcrumbs). Spread the paté on one side, and some sriracha on the other. Add in the cooked mushrooms, cucumber, herbs, chillies and drained pickles and serve.

Jerk-style hen of the woods
with rice and plantain

SERVES 4

DIFFICULTY 🍄🍄

200 g (7 oz) long grain (or basmati) rice
1 x 400 g (14 oz) tin kidney beans in water
¼ tsp ground allspice
500 g (1 lb 2 oz) hen of the woods (maitake mushrooms)
2 ripe plantain, peeled and sliced 1 cm (0.5 in) thick
vegetable oil, for frying
fine salt

JERK MARINADE

1 scotch bonnet chilli (either whole or with seeds removed)
2 tsps ground allspice
4 spring onions (scallions), chopped
4 garlic cloves
2.5 cm (1 in) fresh ginger root
juice of 1 lime
1 tbsp fresh thyme leaves (or 1 tsp dried)
2 tbsps dark brown sugar
2 tsps sea salt flakes
½ tsp ground cinnamon
½ teaspoon ground black pepper

TO SERVE

spring onions (scallions), chopped
jerk sauce

The jerk marinade for this recipe can be made up to five days in advance and kept in the refrigerator. It just gets better day by day. I'm not afraid to condone a shop-bought marinade either – the same recipe would apply to a ready-made jerk paste, in case you do not have time to make it from scratch or access to all the ingredients.

1. Place all the jerk marinade ingredients in a food processor and blitz until smooth.
2. Meanwhile add the rice to a lidded saucepan, along with the whole tin of kidney beans in their water, the allspice and 200 ml (7 fl oz) water. Stir and set over a high heat to bring to the boil. Once boiling, turn down to the lowest heat and cover with a lid. Cook for 10 minutes and then remove from heat but leave the lid on for a further 10 minutes to steam.
3. Add 2 tablespoons of vegetable oil to a large frying pan (skillet) and place the mushroom pieces in a layer in the cold pan and cover with a piece of parchment paper. Then take a large saucepan (one that just fits inside the frying pan) and half-fill it with water (for weight) and place the pan on top of the parchment paper, to press the mushrooms down. Turn the heat up to medium-high.
4. Cook for 5 minutes over a medium heat then remove the pan and parchment paper, and flip the mushrooms over. Add in the jerk marinade, put the paper and saucepan of water back on top and cook for a further 5–10 minutes.

(Continued overleaf)

5. To fry your plantain, take a third pan, fill it with vegetable oil to a depth of 3 cm (1.25 in) and set on a high heat for 4 minutes. Then turn the heat down to low and add the plantain in a single layer (depending on the size of your pan you may need to do this in batches). Fry for 6–8 minutes, stirring and flipping occasionally to stop the pieces sticking to each other or the bottom of the pan. Remove with a slotted spoon and drain on paper towels and season with some fine salt.
6. Serve the jerk mushrooms with the rice and fried plantain in a bowl, topped with a drizzle of shop-bought jerk sauce and a scattering of spring onions.

Porcini and dill soup

SERVES 4

DIFFICULTY

10 g (½ oz) dried porcini
1 bay leaf
1 tsp black peppercorns
2 allspice berries
700 ml (24 fl oz) good-quality vegetable stock
200 g (7 oz) waxy potatoes, peeled and diced
20 g (¾ oz) butter
200 g (7 oz) fresh porcini, sliced (or 20g dried porcini, soaked in boiling water for 30 minutes then drained)
1½ tbsps plain (all-purpose) flour
2 tsps white wine vinegar
salt and pepper
1 tsp caster (superfine) sugar
50 g (2 oz) sour cream
small bunch of dill, chopped

TO SERVE

4 eggs, soft boiled and then halved, or poached
dill sprigs, optional

Mushroom soup is food for the soul. Across Eastern Europe, mushrooms feature heavily, as do soups. Quite often porcini and dill will be matched, sometimes it's chanterelle and marjoram and, in Hungary, it might be paprika and button mushrooms. This particular recipe is based on the dish *kulajda* from the Czech Republic, a traditional South Bohemian soup.

1. Add the dried porcini to a large pan along with the bay leaf, peppercorns, allspice berries and stock. Bring to a gentle simmer for 10 minutes to infuse. Pour through a sieve into a jug and discard the spices.
2. Place the diced potato in a saucepan and cover with cold salted water. Bring to a boil and cook for 8–10 minutes, until tender. Drain and set aside.
3. Heat the butter in a deep sauté pan (or saucepan) and cook the fresh (or dried and prepared) porcini over a medium-high heat for 2–3 minutes until beginning to colour. Take a couple out and set aside for serving. Add the flour to the butter and remaining mushrooms and stir constantly, cooking for 2–3 minutes to ensure there is no raw flour taste.
4. Add the stock to the flour mixture, a little at a time, stirring constantly, until you have added all the stock and it is a thickened soup consistency. Season with salt and pepper and stir in the vinegar, sugar and cooked potatoes.
5. Pour in the cream and warm through but do not boil and, finally, add the chopped dill.
6. Serve the soup in a shallow bowl topped with an egg and the reserved mushrooms, and a few more dill sprigs, if you like.

Shredded king oyster tacos

MAKES 6–8

DIFFICULTY

PICKLED RED ONION

1 small red onion, thinly sliced
50 g (2 oz) caster (superfine) sugar
3 tbsps white wine vinegar
3 tbsps water

CHIPOTLE MUSHROOMS

450 g (1 lb) king oyster mushrooms
1 tbsp vegetable oil
2 tsps chipotle paste
2 tsps agave (or honey)
salt and pepper

GUACAMOLE

2 avocados
juice of 1 lime
sea salt flakes

TO SERVE

6–8 small corn tortillas (12 cm/4.5 in)
cabbage, thinly sliced and seasoned with salt and lime juice
coriander (cilantro)
jalapeño slices (fresh or pickled)
lime wedges

Best enjoyed in the summer sunshine with an ice-cold beer. The smoky savouriness of the mushrooms is really brought to life with all the fresh toppings. This is a vibrant-looking mouthful of food you can really get your hands around. If you like, double up on the pickled onions – they are a delicious addition to many a mushroom meal and keep in the fridge for up to a month.

1. Preheat the oven to 200°C fan (400°F).
2. Start by pickling the red onion. Place the sliced onion in a heatproof bowl. Separately, bring the sugar, vinegar and water to a boil in a small saucepan. As soon as it is boiling, remove from the heat and pour it over the onion. Set aside and leave to pickle.
3. Shred the mushrooms with your hands and add them to a large bowl. Drizzle with the oil and season with salt and pepper and then get your hands in and massage the oil into the mushrooms. Place on a baking tray and cook for 10–15 minutes. Stir together the chipotle and agave and then add that to the mushrooms and mix well. Return to the oven for a further 5 minutes.
4. Meanwhile, make the guacamole by mashing the avocado flesh with a fork in a bowl, adding in the lime juice and salt and stirring together. Alternatively, put it all in a food processor and blitz until smooth.
5. To serve, toast the tortillas on both sides in a hot dry pan and then plate up. Spread a dollop of guacamole on each tortilla, a little cabbage, then add a spoonful of chipotle mushrooms. Drain the pickled red onion and add a few slices to each tortilla. Finish with a scattering of jalapeños and some coriander. Serve with lime wedges on the side.

Shiitake onigiri bento box

MAKES 6 ONIGIRI (FOR 2–3 BENTO BOXES)

DIFFICULTY 🍄🍄

RICE

200 g (7 oz) sushi rice
260 ml (9 fl oz) water
2 tbsps sushi vinegar
1½ tbsps caster (superfine) sugar
1 tsp fine salt
2 spring onions (scallions), green parts only (white parts saved for filling), sliced
2 tsps sesame seeds
1 sheet of nori, cut into 6 rectangles

FILLING

½ tsp vegetable oil
100 g (3½ oz) shiitake mushrooms, diced
2 spring onions (scallions), white parts, sliced
3 tsps teriyaki (or soy) sauce
1 tsp mirin

SUGGESTIONS FOR BUILDING YOUR BENTO BOX

tempura (page 24)
Japanese pickles (of any kind), drained
edamame beans, blanched
lightly dressed salad leaves or vegetables
marinated boiled eggs (page 84)

This is a Japanese bento-style colourful packed lunch. Perfect, portable and ideal for the office or for kids to take to school, and you can adjust the contents to whatever snacky things you might enjoy alongside the onigiri. If you are making it for a child, you could cut some vegetables into star or flower shapes using a cookie cutter and make it all look a little more fun.

1. Wash the rice well until the water runs clear, and drain completely. Place the rice and water into a saucepan (that has a tight-fitting lid) and set over a high heat with the lid off. Bring to a boil then quickly put the lid on the pan and turn the heat down to the lowest possible. Leave to cook very gently for 15 minutes, without removing the lid. After 15 minutes, remove the lid to let steam out and stir the rice, replace the lid and leave for another 10–15 minutes off the heat.
2. Stir the sugar, salt, spring onion greens and sesame seeds through the rice then transfer it to a baking parchment or cling film (plastic wrap) lined tray and leave to cool.
3. Make the mushroom filling. Fry the mushrooms and reserved spring onion in the vegetable oil in a small saucepan over a medium heat for 3–4 minutes. Stir in the teriyaki and mirin for 30 seconds and then remove from the heat and set aside to cool.
4. Once the rice is cool, wet your hands in lightly salted water and divide the rice into 6. Grab one portion and flatten out in your hand. Place one-sixth of the mushroom filling in the middle, then gather up the edges to form a ball. Press into a triangle shape (if you are struggling you can use cling film to help with this whole process). Fold a piece of nori around one edge of the triangle to complete your onigiri. Repeat with the other 5 portions of rice and mushrooms.
5. Fill the bento box with whatever sides you like along with 2–3 onigiri per box. Best served at room temperature within a few of hours, they can be kept in the refrigerator overnight but the rice may be a little less soft the next day.

Creamy wild mushrooms on toast

SERVES 2

DIFFICULTY

knob of butter
1 banana shallot, finely diced
1 garlic clove, sliced
200 g (7 oz) wild mushrooms, such as chanterelles, winter girolles and pied de mouton
1 tbsp Marsala (or sherry), optional
100 ml (3½ fl oz) double (heavy) cream
chives (or tarragon or parsley), finely chopped
squeeze of lemon juice
2 slices sourdough toast
sea salt flakes and freshly ground black pepper

An age-old mushroom classic and a worldwide favourite, this is one of those dishes that will never go out of fashion. You can use absolutely any mushrooms you like. Top with a poached egg, if you're feeling especially hungry.

1. Melt the butter in a large frying pan (skillet) over a medium-high heat and then sauté the shallots for 4–5 minutes until they begin to brown. Add in the garlic and cook for 1 minute more until translucent.
2. Turn the heat up to high and add the mushrooms with a little salt and cook for 3–4 minutes, stirring occasionally, watching carefully that the shallots do not burn.
3. Stir in the Marsala and cook out for a further minute, followed by the cream for just 30 seconds, and then remove the pan from the heat. Finish by stirring through the chopped chives, lemon juice and a good grinding of black pepper.
4. Serve the mushrooms straight away on top of a slice of toasted sourdough.

Crispy hoisin oyster mushroom bao

SERVES 2–3

DIFFICULTY

vegetable oil, for frying
50 g (2 oz) cornflour (cornstarch)
30 g (1 oz) plain (all-purpose) flour
¼ tsp baking powder
pinch of fine salt
100 ml (3½ fl oz) ice-cold water
100 g (3½ oz) oyster mushrooms
100 g (3½ oz) hoisin sauce

FILLING

1 tablespoon sriracha
1 tablespoon mayonnaise
1 tsp freshly squeezed lime juice
75 g (2½ oz) white cabbage, finely sliced

TO SERVE

6 ready-made bao
25 g (1 oz) roasted salted peanuts, crushed
cucumber, sliced
spring onions (scallions), sliced

Bao are fluffy steamed pocket-shaped buns. You can buy ready made in the supermarket and fill them to your heart's content. If you can't find bao, you can still make the same filling and replicate a crispy duck pancake, but with mushrooms! You can make the hoisin mushrooms in advance and warm through at 200°C fan (400°F) for 8–10 minutes.

1. Pour 1 cm (½ in) of oil into a frying pan (skillet) and place over a medium heat to warm.
2. Whisk together the cornflour, flour, baking powder, salt and water until smooth.
3. Check the oil is hot by dropping in a little bit of batter - it should sizzle.
4. Dip the oyster mushrooms into the batter and then lay in a single layer in the oil. Cook for 2–3 minutes on each side and then remove onto paper towel to drain excess oil.
5. Add the crispy mushrooms into a large bowl along with the hoisin sauce and stir to coat.
6. In a bowl, stir together the mayonnaise, sriracha and lime juice. Mix with the cabbage, to coat completely.
7. Warm the buns according to packet instructions and assemble the bao by spooning in the cabbage, topped with the hoisin mushrooms, peanuts, cucumber and spring onions.

Mushroom larb in lettuce cups

SERVES 2

DIFFICULTY

1 tbsp Thai rice (or any rice)
350 g (12 oz) mixed mushrooms (such as oyster and shimeji), roughly chopped
2 tbsps vegetable oil
2 Thai shallots, finely sliced
1 bird's eye chilli, sliced
1 tsp vegan fish sauce
juice of ½ lime
1 tbsp soy sauce
5 g (¼ oz) Thai basil leaves, chopped
5 g (¼ oz) mint leaves, chopped
5 g (¼ oz) coriander (cilantro), chopped

TO SERVE

baby gem leaves
lime wedges
cucumber, sliced
green beans or mangetout (snow peas)
crispy shallots, optional
sticky rice, optional

This warm Thai salad is characterized by the toasted rice powder. Typically made from pork or chicken, this mixed mushroom version is just as tasty and makes for a delicious lunch.

1. Toast the rice in a large dry frying pan (skillet) over a high heat, shaking often, for about 3–4 minutes until lightly golden all over. Tip out of the pan into a bowl and leave to cool.
2. Once cooled, blend in a small food processor or grind in a pestle and mortar until you have a coarse powder and set aside.
3. In the same pan, cook the mushrooms in the vegetable oil for 5–6 minutes over a high heat, then turn the heat off and add the shallots, chilli, fish sauce, lime juice and soy sauce. Stir together to mix and when slightly cooled, stir in the chopped herbs and half the rice powder.
4. Spoon the mushroom mix into the lettuce leaf 'cups' and scatter over the remaining rice powder.
5. Enjoy straight away with fresh vegetables on the side along with some sticky rice, if you like.

Porcini and cheese croquetas

MAKES 20

DIFFICULTY

20 g (¾ oz) dried porcini mushrooms
50 g (2 oz) butter
½ leek, finely chopped
pinch of nutmeg
50 g (2 oz) plain (all-purpose) flour, plus extra for dusting
450 ml (15 fl oz) whole milk
100 g (3½ oz) Manchego, finely grated
2 eggs, beaten
100 g (3½ oz) fine breadcrumbs
vegetable (or olive) oil, for frying
sea salt flakes and freshly ground black pepper

The typical Spanish tapas of *croquetas* is the ideal vehicle for dried mushrooms – their rich flavour perfectly complemented by the cheesy béchamel sauce mixture. A Spanish friend of mine once told me that the best croquetas should have the texture of beautifully creamy mashed potato with not a morsel of potato involved. Note that these require chilling time in advance.

1. Place the porcini in a heatproof bowl and pour over enough boiling water to cover. Leave for 15 minutes to rehydrate and then drain and finely chop.
2. Melt the butter in a saucepan over a medium heat and sauté the leek for 5 minutes until softened. Add in the chopped porcini and cook for a further 5 minutes, stirring often. Mix in the nutmeg and flour and cook for 3–4 minutes, stirring constantly.
3. Add the milk, little by little, stirring between each addition to loosen the mixture. Once all the milk is added bring the mixture to a boil briefly and then take off the heat, stir through the cheese, and season with salt and pepper.
4. Pour the mixture onto a baking tray, cover closely with cling film (plastic wrap) and place in the refrigerator for at least 2 hours or overnight, until completely chilled.
5. When you are ready to assemble your croquetas, generously dust your hands with flour, take a heaped tablespoon of chilled mixture and roll it into a cylinder shape. Repeat until you have used all the mixture. If your room and/or hands are warm you may find the mixture too delicate – you can freeze it for 30 minutes to make it more manageable.
6. Next, roll each piece in the egg and then into the breadcrumbs to coat completely.
7. Now half fill a large saucepan with oil and heat until 180°C (350°F). Fry the breaded croquetas in the oil for 2 minutes until golden brown.
8. Drain on paper towels and eat while warm.

Garlic mushroom tapas

SERVES 2–4

DIFFICULTY

1 shallot, finely diced
1 tsp white wine vinegar
200 g (7 oz) button or chestnut mushrooms
2 tbsps extra virgin olive oil, plus extra for drizzling
2 garlic cloves, chopped
30 g (1 oz) butter
pinch of hot smoked paprika
2 tbsps white wine (or dry sherry)
100 ml (3½ fl oz) vegetable stock
small bunch parsley, chopped
sea salt flakes and freshly ground black pepper
lemon wedges, to serve

A staple on any table of tapas, these garlicky shrooms are great with crusty bread to dunk into the punchy garlic oil. This is a brilliant no-fuss, no-frills dish that will make mouths water when you place it on the table.

1. Place the shallot in a small bowl with the vinegar and a big pinch of salt and set aside.
2. Trim the mushroom stalks to sit flush with the caps, so they cook evenly.
3. Set a sauté pan over a medium heat and add the oil and mushrooms along with a pinch of salt and cook for 2 minutes on each side. Then add in the garlic, butter, paprika and shallot mixture and cook for a further minute to soften.
4. Pour in the white wine to deglaze the pan and then add the vegetable stock. Bubble away over a low heat for 4–5 minutes until the liquid has reduced by about half.
5. Remove from the heat, stir through the parsley and season with salt and pepper.
6. Serve warm, topped with a hefty drizzle more of olive oil and a wedge of lemon.

Meatless meatballs in tomato sauce

MAKES 12

DIFFICULTY 🍄🍄

1 tbsp olive oil, plus extra for drizzling
200 g (7 oz) chestnut or button mushrooms, roughly chopped
½ onion, chopped
1 garlic clove, chopped
75 g (2½ oz) rolled oats
1 egg
½ tsp smoked paprika
½ tsp dried oregano
small bunch of parsley, chopped, plus extra to serve
25 g (1 oz) Manchego, finely grated

TOMATO SAUCE

1 tbsp olive oil
½ onion, finely chopped
1 garlic clove, chopped
3 tbsps red (or white) wine
1 x 400 g (14 oz) tin finely chopped tomatoes
200 ml (7 fl oz) water
1 tsp caster (superfine) sugar

You can serve these as a tapas dish, with bread and aioli on the side, or on top of spaghetti with a generous grating of cheese. As part of a tapas spread, they pair very well with Garlic mushrooms (page 63) and Porcini and cheese croquetas (page 62).

1. Preheat the oven to 200°C (400°F).
2. To make the meatballs, in a large pan fry the mushrooms in the olive oil over a medium heat for 4–5 minutes, until they have decreased in size by about half and the moisture has evaporated. Add the onion and garlic and cook for 4–5 minutes more. Remove from the heat and leave to cool slightly. Once cooled, transfer to a food processor along with the oats, egg, paprika, oregano and parsley. Blitz together until it is a uniform texture but not completely smooth, then stir through the grated Manchego.
3. Divide this mixture into 12 and gently shape into balls. Place onto a lined baking tray and drizzle with a little oil. Cook in the oven for 10–12 minutes until firm.
4. For the tomato sauce, wipe down the mushroom pan and add the olive oil. Sweat the onion for 8–10 minutes then add garlic and cook for another minute until fragrant. Deglaze the pan by adding in the wine and then cook to reduce the liquid by half. Add in the tomatoes and water and cook for 10–15 minutes.
5. Add the meatballs into the tomato sauce and stir to coat.
6. Serve warm, scattered with parsley.

Top left: Garlic mushroom tapas (page 63)
Top right: Meatless meatballs in tomato sauce (page 64)
Bottom: Porcini and cheese croquetas (page 62)

Baked mushroom shawarma

SERVES 4

DIFFICULTY

BAKED MUSHROOMS
250 g (9 oz) oyster mushrooms
250 g (9 oz) king oyster mushrooms
4 tbsps extra virgin olive oil
2 tsps ground cumin
1 tsp smoked paprika
¼ tsp ground cinnamon
1 tsp ground coriander (cilantro)
2 garlic cloves, crushed
sea salt flakes and freshly ground black pepper

SUMAC ONIONS
1 red onion, sliced
1 tsp white wine vinegar
2 tsps sumac
small bunch of parsley, leaves only, chopped

TAHINI YOGHURT
2 tbsps tahini
75 g (2½ oz) Greek yoghurt
juice of ½ lemon
1–3 tbsps water

TO SERVE
4 flatbreads
hummus
pickled chillies, turnips and gherkins, optional

A low-effort, high-reward lunch, full of flavour, this recipe is inspired by Middle-Eastern shawarma but swaps out the spit for the oven and meat for mushrooms. You could buy a premade shawarma spice mix if you prefer. This makes for a great summer lunch with friends in the garden – bring it all out in bowls so everyone can pile up their own flatbread according to their preference.

1. Preheat the oven to 200°C fan (400°F).
2. Tear the mushrooms into strips and add them to a large bowl with the oil, cumin, paprika, cinnamon, coriander, garlic, salt and pepper. Use your hands to massage the marinade into the mushrooms and then transfer to a baking tray. Place in the oven to roast for 15–20 minutes until golden and a little crispy, tossing halfway through.
3. For the sumac onions, mix the onion, vinegar, sumac, parsley and some salt and pepper together and set aside.
4. Make the tahini yogurt by mixing all the ingredients together in a bowl, and depending on the thickness of your yoghurt, loosen it with 1–3 tablespoons of water.
5. To assemble, spread a dollop of hummus on the base of each flatbread, top with the cooked mushrooms, a scattering of sumac onions, a drizzle of tahini yoghurt and, finally, pickles, to your liking.

BOWLS OF COMFORT

These hearty dinner recipes are meals you can really sink into. They could otherwise be described as a hug in a bowl in all its different forms, from noodles to curries, salads to soups. Where a mushroom feels comfortable, so do we.

Black trompette pappardelle

with egg yolks

SERVES 2

DIFFICULTY

250 g (9 oz) pappardelle
80 g (3 oz) butter
2 banana shallots, finely chopped
150 g (5 oz) black trumpet mushrooms (or chanterelles/girolles)
60 g (2 oz) pecorino, finely grated, plus extra to serve
large handful of parsley leaves, chopped
2 egg yolks
sea salt flakes and freshly ground black pepper

This modern Italian plate sees ribbons of pasta served in a silky sauce. It is so simple to knock together but ends up a deliciously rich and indulgent dish – perfect for date night or cooking and enjoying with someone you love. A large handful of chopped parsley is important here as the herb's grassy notes are comforting to the woody flavour of autumnal mushrooms and bring this dish to life.

1. Bring a large pan of salted water to the boil, cook the pappardelle according to the packet instructions and then drain (but reserve the pasta water).
2. Meanwhile, in a separate large frying pan (skillet), melt half the butter over a medium heat and sauté the shallots for 4–5 minutes until softened. Increase the heat to high and add in the mushrooms, cooking for 5–6 minutes until wilted and caramelized.
3. Add a ladle of the pasta water to the mushroom mix and shake the pan vigorously (or stir quickly), to emulsify and thicken the sauce, then add the grated cheese and the rest of the butter and season with salt and pepper.
4. Stir the drained pasta into the mushrooms and shake (or stir). Loosen the sauce a little more by adding another 100 ml (3½ fl oz) of reserved pasta water. Add the chopped parsley and mix well.
5. Remove from the heat and serve topped with an egg yolk and lots more grated cheese and eat immediately.

Thai green curry

SERVES 4

DIFFICULTY

2 tbsps vegetable oil
150 g (5 oz) button (or chestnut) mushrooms, halved (quartered if using chestnuts)
200 g (7 oz) aubergine (eggplant), cubed
400 ml (13 fl oz) coconut milk
200 ml (7 fl oz) water
2 tsps soy sauce
2 kaffir lime leaves
150 g (5 oz) mangetout (snow peas)
100g (3½ oz) bamboo shoots

CURRY PASTE

1 lemongrass stalk, outer leaves removed, and centre chopped
2 shallots
2 garlic cloves
2 tsps galangal paste
4 green chillies, chopped
zest of 1 lime
1 tsp cumin seeds
1 tsp coriander (cilantro) seeds
1 tsp vegan fish sauce
2 tsp soft light brown sugar

TO SERVE

jasmine rice
coriander (cilantro)
Thai basil
red bird's eye chilli, sliced
lime wedges

We're spicing things up with this curry. It's perfect when you want something comforting, nourishing and hot! The curry paste has a deeply flavoured citrusy goodness and the mushrooms absorb it all, like the beautiful sponges that they are.

1. Blend all the curry paste ingredients together in a food processor until completely smooth. If your blender is struggling, you can add 1–2 tablespoons of the coconut milk to help it along.
2. For the curry, heat the oil in a sauté pan or wok and add your curry paste. Cook over a medium heat for 5–6 minutes, stirring occasionally at first then leave undisturbed until the oil separates and comes to the top. Add in the mushrooms and aubergine and coat them in the curry paste, cooking and stirring for 2–3 minutes.
3. Add the coconut milk, water, soy sauce and kaffir lime leaves and bring to a gentle simmer. Turn the heat to low and simmer for 20 minutes, until the aubergine is cooked and the oil has again split at the surface. If the liquid has reduced too much you can add a little more water. Add in the mangetout and bamboo shoots and simmer for 2 minutes more.
4. Serve the curry with some jasmine rice and garnish with coriander, Thai basil, a few slices of chilli and a good squeeze of lime.

Miso and walnut udon noodle bowl with shiitake and shimeji

SERVES 4

DIFFICULTY

4 portions of udon noodles (dried or frozen)
150 g (5 oz) mixed mushrooms (such as oyster, shiitake and shimeji), sliced
150 g (5 oz) sweetheart/hispi cabbage, roughly chopped

BROTH

1.2 litres (40 fl oz) vegetarian dashi
1 piece of kombu
4 dried shiitake mushrooms
3 tbsps soy sauce
2 tbsps mirin
1 tbsp soft light brown sugar

WALNUT MISO

125 g (4 oz) walnut pieces
1½ tbsp soft light brown sugar
½ tbsp boiling water
1 tbsp red miso paste
1 tbsp white miso paste
1 tsp mirin

2 spring onions (scallions), green part only, sliced, to serve

This dish is inspired by Koya, objectively speaking London's best udon counter-eatery. A concentration of powerful flavours in the umami-rich walnut and miso paste brings some great depth to this warming noodle bowl. A soulful, rich, comforting dish ready for slurping! I like to serve the walnut paste on the side for the diner to add in as they go.

1. Preheat the oven to 170°C fan (340°F).
2. First make the broth by heating the dashi, kombu and dried shiitake in a large saucepan until boiling. Once boiling, turn the heat down to low and infuse for at least 30 minutes (you can do this in advance and then keep the cold broth in the refrigerator). Remove the kombu and shiitake and discard. Stir in the soy sauce, mirin and sugar and taste for seasoning (you do not want it to be too salty as the miso paste will be a salty kick). Add a little more water if your broth has reduced.
3. For the walnut miso, roast the walnuts on a tray for 10–12 minutes until they smell toasted. Place onto a clean tea towel and rub to brush off as much skin as possible. Grind the walnuts using a pestle and mortar or a food processor, until they are roughly ground but still have some texture.
4. Next, mix the sugar and the boiling water together in a medium bowl and stir for 30 seconds until the sugar is dissolved. Add in both miso pastes and the mirin and stir in the ground toasted walnuts. Divide the walnut miso paste between 4 small sauce pots or ramekins.
5. Cook the udon noodles according to the packet instructions and divide between four deep bowls.
6. Bring the broth to a gentle boil, add in the mixed mushrooms and cabbage and simmer for 4–5 minutes.
7. To serve, ladle the broth, mushrooms and cabbage over the noodles and garnish with spring onions. Serve the walnut miso paste on the side to add as you eat.

King oyster biryani

SERVES 4

DIFFICULTY

250 ml (8½ fl oz) vegetable oil
4 onions, finely sliced
200 g (7 oz) Greek yoghurt
1 tbsp garlic paste
1 tbsp ginger paste
2 tsps garam masala
1 tsps chilli powder
1 tsp ground turmeric
1 tsp sea salt flakes
1 tbsp tomato purée (paste)
juice of ½ a lime
400 g (14 oz) king oyster mushrooms, roughly chopped, or a mixture of mushrooms such as chestnut, oyster and king oyster
3 tomatoes, quartered
300 g (10½ oz) basmati rice
450 ml (15 fl oz) water
1 bay leaf
5 cardamom pods
pinch of saffron

TO SERVE

coriander (cilantro), chopped
pomegranate seeds, optional
yoghurt (or raita)

My friend Priyanka taught me how to make biriyani when we would cook masalas together in our university days and I have adapted her chicken biriyani recipe to make this mushroom version. You can use any mushrooms suggested for this – but I like king oyster for their springy yet firm texture. This is even more delicious heated through the next day.

1. Start by heating the vegetable oil in a large heavy-bottomed pan and once it is about 170°C (340°F), carefully add in the onions and cook at a medium heat for 15–25 minutes, stirring very occasionally, until golden brown. Then pour them into a colander over a heatproof bowl to drain off the excess oil.
2. Next, in a large bowl, mix the yoghurt, garlic and ginger pastes, garam masala, chilli powder, turmeric, salt, tomato purée and lime juice. Add in the mushrooms and half the cooked onions and mix well.
3. Add 1 tablespoon of the frying oil (and safely discard the rest once cool) into a 20 cm (8 in) pan over a medium heat. Tip in the mushrooms with all their marinade. Cook for 10–12 minutes, stirring often, and then add the tomatoes and cook for 5 minutes more. If the mixture catches on the bottom of the pan, add a splash of water.
4. Meanwhile, add the rice, water, bay leaf, cardamom and saffron to a small saucepan. Bring to a boil over a high heat and as soon as the rice is boiling, turn down to low and cover with a lid or tightly fitted foil. Cook for 7 minutes then turn off the heat and remove the lid.
5. Reduce the heat of the mushrooms to the lowest possible and then add the par-boiled rice to the pan in a layer on top of the mushroom mix. Add the remaining fried onions on top and then cover with a lid, or tightly with foil, and cook for 10–15 minutes (depending on how low you can get your heat).
6. Top with coriander to serve, a sprinkling of pomegranate seeds, if using, and some yoghurt on the side.

Mushroom tikka masala

SERVES 4

DIFFICULTY

4 tsps garam masala
½–1 tsp chilli powder (depending on how spicy you like things)
4 tsps tandoori masala
100 g (3½ oz) plain yoghurt
1 tbsp garlic paste
1 tbsp ginger paste
1 tbsp vegetable oil
juice of ½ lemon
350 g (12 oz) button mushrooms, halved
225 g (8 oz) paneer, cubed

CURRY SAUCE

3 tbsp ghee (or vegetable oil)
2 onions, chopped
1 tbsp garlic paste
1 tbsp ginger paste
1 tbsp tomato purée (paste)
2 tsps dried fenugreek leaves
300 g (10½ oz) passata
300 ml (10 fl oz) water
150 ml (5 fl oz) double (heavy) cream

TO SERVE

coriander (cilantro)
fresh ginger root, cut into matchsticks
steamed rice
chapatis

Get cosy with this familiar dish – this time using mushrooms and paneer instead of meat. Curry leftovers always taste good, so do not hesitate to make a bigger batch than you need. Best served with rice and chapatis and eaten on your sofa in front of a movie on a Sunday evening.

1. Preheat the grill (broiler) to high.
2. Mix the garam masala, chilli powder and tandoori masala together for the spice mix and toast in a dry frying pan (skillet). Set over a medium heat for 1–2 minutes, shaking the pan frequently, until fragrant. Tip half into a large bowl and half onto a plate.
3. Next, add the yoghurt, garlic and ginger pastes, oil and lemon juice to the spice mix in the bowl. Add the mushrooms and paneer and stir to coat them in the marinade. Leave to sit for at least 20 minutes while you prepare the curry sauce.
4. For the sauce, heat the ghee in a large sauté pan and fry off the onion for 10–12 minutes over a medium-high heat until softened. Add in the other half of the spice mix and fry for 1–2 minutes until fragrant, before adding the garlic and ginger pastes for 1–2 minutes. Add the tomato purée and fenugreek leaves and fry for 1 minute and then the passata along with the water. Reduce the heat to low and cook for 10–15 minutes, stirring occasionally. Use a hand-held blender to blend the sauce until completely smooth and then stir through the cream.
5. Meanwhile, place the marinated mushrooms and paneer on a tray and grill for 8–10 minutes until charred at the edges, then add into the curry sauce and warm the whole thing through for 2 minutes.
6. Serve straight away with rice and a chapati, and top with some fresh coriander and sliced ginger.

Wood ear Vietnamese spring rolls with noodle salad and nuoc mam sauce

SERVES 4

DIFFICULTY

25 g (1 oz) dried wood ear mushrooms
50 g (2 oz) rice noodles, cooked, cooled and roughly chopped
60 g (2 oz) carrot, finely chopped
60 g (2 oz) daikon (mooli), finely chopped
4 spring onions (scallions), finely chopped
60 g (2 oz) beansprouts, finely chopped
1 tsp mushroom seasoning (or ½ tsp salt)
12–16 spring roll rice papers
vegetable oil, for deep-frying

DIPPING SAUCE

3 tbsps vegan fish sauce
Juice of 1 lime
4 tbsps boiling water
3 tbsps caster (superfine) sugar
2 garlic cloves, chopped
1–2 red bird's eye chillies, finely sliced

TO SERVE

4 portions vermicelli noodles
lettuce leaves
coriander (cilantro), whole stems
mint leaves
cucumber, sliced
carrot and daikon pickle (page 46)
chopped peanuts

You can buy wood ear mushrooms dried or fresh but dried are easier to source and have the added benefit of keeping for longer. The texture and bite of these spring rolls makes for a really satisfying bowl of food while the vegetables keep it fresh and vibrant. If you do not fancy all the hand chopping, you can put the spring roll filling into a food processor to finely chop, just make sure it doesn't turn to mush.

1. Pour boiling water over the dried mushrooms and soak for at least 30 minutes, or overnight. Once soaked, drain and finely chop the mushrooms and place in a large bowl.
2. Add the rice noodles, carrot, daikon, spring onions, beansprouts and seasoning to the wood ear mushrooms and mix well.
3. Fill a baking tray (pan) with warm water. Working one at a time, dunk a spring roll rice paper into the water for 1 second and then place it onto a flat surface. Spoon 2 heaped tablespoons of the mushroom filling onto the bottom third of the rice paper then fold the two sides in and roll up tightly into a spring roll, starting from the edge closest you. Repeat with the rest of the ingredients to make 12–16 spring rolls.
4. Make the dipping sauce by stirring together all the ingredients in a bowl until the sugar has dissolved.
5. Half fill a heavy-bottomed pan with vegetable oil and heat to 180°C (350°F).
6. Cook the spring rolls in the heated oil in batches, for 4–6 minutes until crispy all over (some rice papers will go golden brown, others will stay white). Remove the rolls from the oil onto a wire rack, to drain any excess.
7. When cool enough to handle, cut the spring rolls in half and serve straight away on a bed of noodles with lettuce leaves, herbs and cucumber on the side and finish with a spoonful of carrot and daikon pickle and a scattering of chopped peanuts. Serve the dipping sauce on the side or poured all over the dish.

Mushroom bourguignon

SERVES 4

DIFFICULTY

1 tbsp vegetable oil
20 round shallots, peeled whole
15 g (½ oz) butter
500 g (1 lb 2 oz) mixed mushrooms (chestnut and wild mushrooms), larger chopped in half, smaller left whole
2 garlic cloves, sliced
1 tbsp tomato purée (paste)
3 tbsps plain (all-purpose) flour
500 ml (17 fl oz) vegetable stock
350 ml (12 fl oz) red wine
1 tsp vegan Worcestershire sauce
100 g (3½ oz) pre-cooked chestnuts, halved
2 bay leaves
sprig of rosemary
2 carrots, peeled and roughly chopped
sea salt flakes and freshly ground black pepper

TO SERVE

mashed potatoes or Porcini and potato gratin (page 134)
chives or parsley, chopped

A hearty dish perfect for a wintry evening. It's best served over mashed potatoes or with another potato side dish, but also makes a great pie filling when topped with a suet crust (see the Morel, leek and tarragon pie recipe on page 103).

Mushrooms are often found growing at the base of trees such as chestnuts, oaks and pines. There is a phrase used when talking about seasonal cooking, 'what grows together, goes together', and I am going to apply it here – perhaps mushrooms and chestnuts do go together so beautifully because they grow together.

1. Preheat the oven to 180°C fan (350°F).
2. Heat the oil in an ovenproof casserole dish (Dutch oven) over a high heat, add in the whole shallots and brown for 5–6 minutes before adding the butter and mushrooms to brown for 4–5 minutes. Add the garlic and cook for 1 minute before adding the tomato purée and the flour. Stir constantly for a minute to cook the flour through, then pour in the stock, a little at time, stirring to get rid of any lumps. Add the wine, Worcestershire sauce, chestnuts, bay leaves, rosemary and carrots, season with salt and pepper and bring to the boil.
3. Place into the oven, lid off, for 35–40 minutes until the sauce is thickened and the carrots and shallots are cooked through.
4. Enjoy hot, scattered with chives or parsley, with your favourite type of potatoes on the side.

Ramen with shiitake and soy-marinated eggs

SERVES 4

DIFFICULTY

SOY-MARINATED EGGS
1 tbsp mirin
3 tbsps dark soy sauce
1 piece kombu
1 dried shiitake mushroom
125 ml (4 fl oz) boiling water
4 eggs

BROTH
1 tsp vegetable oil
2 cm (1 in) fresh ginger root, chopped
2 garlic cloves, chopped
1 tbsp white or red miso
1 litre (34 fl oz) ramen broth
1 tbsp soy sauce, optional
200 g (7 oz) shiitake mushrooms, caps scored or halved

TOPPINGS
tofu (pan-fried, then sliced)
2 pak choi, quartered
4 portions of ramen or instant noodles, cooked
nori sheets
4 spring onions (scallions), finely sliced
sesame seeds or Japanese seven spice, optional

It's often said that we eat with our eyes first, and ramen is one of those dishes that is just so pleasing on the eye. You can finish your bowl off with so many delicious things, including vegetables such as tenderstem broccoli, edamame or spinach, and other toppings such as kimchi, chilli oil or coriander. Here, the mushrooms could be pan-fried instead of cooked in the broth. It's your bowl – go wild and make it your own.

1. Start by making the marinated eggs. Make a marinade by placing the mirin, soy sauce, kombu and dried shiitake into a heatproof bowl, pour over the boiling water and leaving to sit.
2. Bring a small pan of water to the boil and add in the eggs. Cook for 6 minutes. Drain and then run the eggs under the cold tap for 1 minute to stop them cooking further. Peel the eggs and add them whole into the marinade. Leave to sit for at least 30 minutes (you can do this step up to 2 days in advance and keep in the refrigerator).
3. To make the soup base, first heat the oil in a large saucepan, add the ginger and garlic and fry for 1–2 minutes until translucent, before stirring through the miso. Add half the ramen broth and use a hand-held blender to blitz, then pass the liquid through a fine sieve into a large pan and add the rest of the broth.
4. Add the mushrooms to the broth and simmer for 3–5 minutes.
5. Meanwhile, pan-fry the tofu for 3 minutes on each side then slice into pieces.
6. Blanch the pak choi in boiling water for 3 minutes.
7. To serve, add the noodles to deep serving bowls and pour in the broth. Arrange the mushrooms, sliced tofu, pak choi, marinated egg, nori and spring onions on top. Scatter with sesame seeds or Japanese seven spice if you like and dig in.

Tom yum soup

SERVES 4

DIFFICULTY

1½ litres (51 fl oz) water
4 dried shiitake mushrooms
8 Thai shallots, peeled and halved
1 lemongrass stalk, bashed
1–2 tsps galangal paste
2 kaffir lime leaves
1–3 tbsps Thai chilli paste (or vegan Tom Yum paste), depending on how spicy you like it
1 tbsp soft light brown sugar
2 tbsps vegan fish sauce
8 cherry tomatoes, halved
250 g (9 oz) shimeji mushrooms
100 g (3 ½ oz) tofu, cubed
1 tbsp lime juice
175 ml (6 fl oz) evaporated coconut milk (or condensed coconut milk and omit the sugar), optional

TO SERVE

lime slices
coriander (cilantro)

Unconventionally, turn this classic soup into a heartier dinner meal by simply adding 100 g (3½ oz) of rice noodles per person for the final 5 minutes of cooking. If you are making the creamy version by adding in the coconut milk, you can keep the rest of the can in the fridge to make a delicious iced latte (page 146).

1. Pour the water into a large saucepan along with the dried mushrooms, shallots, lemongrass, galangal and lime leaves, and bring to a gentle simmer. Cook for 10 minutes.
2. Add the chilli paste, sugar, fish sauce and tomatoes and bring to a very gentle boil again. Stir to mix.
3. Add the mushrooms and tofu and simmer gently for a final 5 minutes, then remove from the heat and stir in the lime juice. Remove the lemongrass and lime leaves and discard.
4. If you'd like to make this a creamy version of the soup, add the coconut milk now and warm through.
5. Serve the soup hot, topped with some slices of lime and fresh coriander.

Shiitake yaki soba

SERVES 4

DIFFICULTY

550 g (1 lb 3½ oz) soba noodles
2 tbsps vegetable oil
1 onion, sliced
150 g (5 oz) shiitake mushrooms, sliced
4 spring onions (scallions), roughly chopped
1 carrot, cut into matchsticks
200 g (7 oz) Chinese cabbage, roughly chopped
200 g (7 oz) bean sprouts

SAUCE

1 tsp vegan Worcestershire sauce
4 tbsps soy sauce
2 tbsps mushroom oyster sauce
1 tbsp ketchup
1 tbsp sesame oil
1 tbsp mirin
1 tbsp sake
½ tsp kombu dashi powder, optional
¼ tsp white pepper

TO SERVE

50 g (2 oz) pickled ginger
sesame seeds, optional
Japanese seven spice, optional

If you prep all the ingredients first, this savoury and satisfying midweek staple takes just 10 minutes to throw together in a pan. It also has the fridge-clearing flexibility of taking many a vegetable with it - you can add in whatever you may need to use up.

1. To make the sauce, simply stir together all the ingredients in a bowl or jug and set aside.
2. For the noodles, start by cooking the soba noodles according to packet instructions, then drain, rinse under cold water until cool and set aside.
3. Next, heat the oil in a large frying pan (skillet) or wok over a high heat for a couple of minutes. Add the onion and mushrooms and stir-fry for 2–3 minutes until beginning to brown. Then add the spring onion, carrot, cabbage and bean sprouts and stir-fry for a further 3–4 minutes.
4. Add the cooked noodles to the pan and stir-fry for 1–2 minutes more before pouring in the sauce and heating it through.
5. Serve hot, topped with pickled ginger, sesame seeds and Japanese seven spice, if desired.

Marry-me mushrooms

with crusty bread

SERVES 2–4

DIFFICULTY

2 tbsps extra virgin olive oil
2 shallots, finely diced
2 garlic cloves, crushed
300 g (10½ oz) button (or chestnut) mushrooms, sliced
15 g (½ oz) butter
1 tbsp tomato purée (paste)
80 g (3 oz) sundried tomatoes, finely chopped
50 ml (1¾ fl oz) vodka
100 ml (3½ fl oz) double (heavy) cream
100 g (3½ oz) baby spinach, optional
sea salt flakes and freshly ground black pepper

TO SERVE

basil leaves
crusty bread

With added vodka, for luck! This recipe is so named because whoever you cook this for is going to want to put a ring on your finger! You can enjoy these mushrooms as they are, with crusty bread dunked in, or stirred through pasta, such as orzo, for a tomatoey, creamy bowl of love.

1. Heat the oil in a large frying pan (skillet) over a medium heat and fry the shallots for 4–5 minutes until softened, then add in the garlic and cook for 1–2 minutes until fragrant.
2. Add the mushrooms, season with salt and pepper and cook for 4–5 minutes until they have wilted, then add the butter and sauté for 1–2 minutes before adding in the tomato purée and sundried tomatoes. Cook for 1–2 minutes more, until just beginning to stick on the bottom of the pan, and then deglaze with the vodka and let the mixture bubble away.
3. Pour in the cream and simmer gently for 5 minutes, until thickened slightly. Then stir through the spinach, if using, and remove the pan from the heat.
4. Serve warm, topped with a few basil leaves, with crusty bread on the side, to someone you want to marry.

Mushroom and chickpea rendang

SERVES 4

DIFFICULTY 🍄🍄🍄

4 tbsps desiccated coconut
4 tbsps vegetable oil
300 g (5 oz) button mushrooms, sliced
2 kaffir lime leaves
400 ml (13 fl oz) coconut milk
1 tsp sugar
1 tsp sea salt
1½ tbsps tamarind paste
1 x 400 g (14 oz) tin chickpeas (garbanzos), drained

SPICE PASTE

5–10 dried chillies, soaked in boiling water for 5 minutes, then drained (or 1–2 tbsps sambal)
2 lemongrass stalks, outer tough layers removed
8 Thai shallots
6 garlic cloves
1½ tsps galangal paste
5 cm (2 in) fresh ginger root
5 cm (2 in) fresh turmeric (or ½ tsp turmeric powder)

PICKLED VEGETABLES

1 tbsp rice vinegar
1 tbsp sugar
1 tsp sambal (or chilli paste), optional
1 carrot, chopped
½ cucumber, sliced

TO SERVE

jasmine rice
crispy shallots, optional

Most commonly made with beef or chicken, this Indonesian-spiced coconut curry is a hearty, flavoursome dish that works beautifully with mushrooms and chickpeas. Choose the quantity of dried chillies according to your level of spice preference and serve with rice.

1. Toast the coconut in a dry pan over a medium heat for 2–3 minutes, stirring constantly, until browned all over. Quickly, before it burns, tip it into a pestle and mortar or food processor and blend or grind until you have a paste. Transfer to a bowl and set aside.
2. To make the spice paste, add all the ingredients into the pestle and mortar or food processor (you do not need to clean it after the coconut). Grind for a few minutes until you have a paste. If your blender is struggling, you can add 1–2 tablespoons of coconut milk to help it along.
3. Next, heat the oil in a large sauté pan or deep frying pan (skillet), add your spice paste and cook for 10–12 minutes over a medium heat, stirring often until the oil has separated. Add the mushrooms and fry off in the paste for 5 minutes until beginning to wilt (if you notice the paste starting to burn then add the coconut milk in and scrape the bottom of the pan to ensure it does not catch). Add the lime leaves, coconut milk, sugar, salt and tamarind and bring to a gentle simmer. Cook over a low heat for 30 minutes, stirring occasionally, then add the chickpeas and cook for a further 5–10 minutes, until you have a thick consistency.
4. Meanwhile, make the pickled vegetables by stirring together the vinegar, sugar and sambal, if using. Add the carrot and cucumber and stir to mix.
5. Returning to the curry, remove the lime leaves and stir in the toasted coconut. Serve straight away, with jasmine rice, pickles on the side and topped with some crispy shallots, if you like.

Green goddess soba salad bowl

SERVES 2

DIFFICULTY 🍄

1 tbsp olive oil
150 g (5 oz) button mushrooms, sliced
60 ml (2 fl oz) vegetable stock
1 tsp vegan Worcestershire sauce
1 tsp maple syrup
200 g (7 oz) soba noodles, cooked (or cooked barley/ farro)
½ avocado, sliced
100 g (3½ oz) cucumber, sliced
1 romaine (or gem) lettuce, shredded
100 g (3½ oz) edamame beans (or mangetout/ snow peas), blanched
100 g (3½ oz) asparagus, blanched
1 spring onion (scallion), chopped, optional
sea salt flakes and freshly ground pepper
black sesame seeds, to serve

DRESSING

3 tbsps mayonnaise
juice of ½ lime
½ avocado
20 g (¾ oz) mixture of fresh herbs (such as parsley, chervil, mint, chives, dill and tarragon)
1 tsp Dijon mustard
½ green chilli, optional
1 tbsp white miso
2 tbsps water
sea salt flakes and freshly ground black pepper

When you think of mushrooms, it would be fairly safe to assume that you don't immediately associate them with salad. However, an umami-flavoured pan-fried mushroom goes so perfectly with this fresh herby green goddess salad dressing that who knows, you might just start matching mushrooms and salad in your mind!

1. First, make the dressing. Blend all of the dressing ingredients together in a high-powered food processor and blend until smooth and uniform in colour.
2. Heat the oil in a frying pan (skillet) over a medium heat, add the mushrooms and some salt and pepper and sauté for 6–7 minutes. Then add the stock, Worcestershire sauce and maple syrup and cook for 1–2 minutes more.
3. To plate up the salad, take a large serving bowl and arrange the soba noodles, sliced avocado, cucumber, lettuce, edamame, asparagus, mushrooms and spring onion neatly. Top with the sesame seeds, and serve the dressing in a little bowl on the side so that each diner can spoon it over and mix together their own salad after they've enjoyed the aesthetics of this beautiful bowl.

CHEESY CREAMY DREAMY

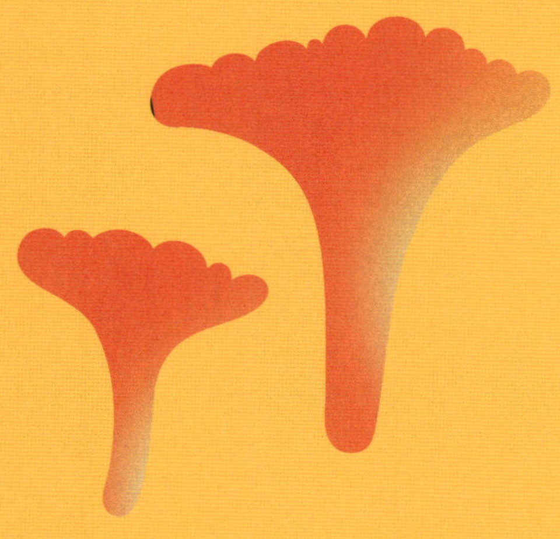

It's no secret how well cheese goes with mushrooms. A reliable combination that I only wish I had come up with. I am simply the middleman of turning these flavour combinations into dishes you can enjoy. These recipes do not shy away from garlicky, creamy, cheesy unapologetic mushroomy richness.

Four cheese pizza bianca

with radicchio and chestnut mushrooms

MAKES 1 PIZZA, EASY TO DOUBLE UP

DIFFICULTY

1 x 220 g (8 oz) ready-made pizza dough
semolina or plain (all-purpose) flour, for dusting
60 g (2 oz) ricotta
30 g (1 oz) crème fraîche
15 g (½ oz) pecorino, finely grated
pinch of chilli flakes
2 radicchio leaves, torn into pieces
1 pickled walnut, sliced, optional
2 chestnut mushrooms, very finely sliced
60 g (2 oz) mozzarella, sliced
60 g (2 oz) Cornish Brie (or Camembert), sliced
extra virgin olive oil
sea salt flakes and freshly ground black pepper

This is so simple to put together: a delicious, filling meal with a ready-made dough and a mixture of cheeses. I think Brie or Camembert works deliciously here with the mushrooms, but if you have blue or goat's cheese, you can use that instead.

1. Preheat the oven to 220°C fan (430°F) and heat a pizza stone or large heavy-bottomed tray on the middle shelf for at least 30 minutes.
2. Flour the work surface and roll the pizza dough out to about 30 cm (12 in). Place on a cold baking sheet or a piece of baking paper.
3. Mix the ricotta, crème fraîche, pecorino and chilli flakes together and season with salt and pepper. Spread the ricotta mix all over the pizza base.
4. Top with the radicchio, pickled walnut (if using), mushroom slices, mozzarella and Brie. Drizzle all over with olive oil.
5. Remove the hot pizza stone or tray from the oven, carefully transfer the pizza to the stone or tray.
6. Cook in the hot oven for 12–14 minutes then slice and enjoy warm.

Chanterelle, cheddar and potato pithivier

SERVES 4–6

DIFFICULTY

500 g (1 lb 2 oz) waxy potatoes (such as Charlotte or Desiree), peeled and finely sliced
1 garlic clove, sliced
½ small onion, very finely sliced
2 tbsps double (heavy) cream
15 g (½ oz) butter
1 small leek, thinly sliced
1 bay leaf
1 thyme sprig
250 g (9 oz) chanterelles, roughly sliced
60 ml (2 fl oz) dry white wine
1½ tsps Dijon (or wholegrain) mustard
2 x 320 g (11 oz) sheets of puff pastry
200 g (9 oz) mature Cheddar cheese, sliced
2 egg yolks
sea salt flakes and freshly ground black pepper

Cheesy potatoey filling accompanying the sweet chanterelles between two layers of puff pastry. A deliciously rich table centrepiece. Best served with a lightly dressed leafy green salad (such as the one on page 118) and best to schedule in a lie down after you've finished.

1. Boil the potatoes in salted water for 8–10 minutes then drain and place into a bowl with the garlic, onion and double cream. Season with salt and pepper and stir then leave to cool completely.
2. Melt the butter in a large frying pan (skillet) and add in the leek, bay leaf and thyme. Season with salt and cook for 5–6 minutes over a medium heat until the leek has softened then add in the chanterelles and cook for 8 minutes until the moisture has evaporated and they are just beginning to caramelize. Deglaze with white wine and cook for 1 minute then remove from the heat, stir in the mustard and season with pepper. Remove the bay leaf and thyme stalk and leave to cool completely.
3. Roll out one of the sheets of pastry and use a 20 cm (8 in) plate as a template to cut round. Roll out the second sheet of pastry and use a 23 cm (9 in) plate as a template to cut round (you can freeze the offcuts for Vol-au-vents, page 26).
4. Place the smaller of the circles onto a piece of baking paper and top with the cooled potato mix, in a circle leaving a 2 cm (0.75 in) border around the edge. Then add a layer of the sliced cheese and top with a domed layer of the chanterelle and leek mix.

(Continued overleaf)

5. Brush the border with egg yolk and then carefully place the larger circle of pastry over the top. Press down to seal at the edges and then brush the whole thing in egg yolk. If time allows, chill the pithivier in the fridge for 30 minutes (or overnight) then brush with egg yolk for a second time.
6. Preheat the oven to 200°C fan (400°F) and preheat a baking tray.
7. Score the top of the pastry lightly with a sharp knife, in crescent shaped lines, from the centre to the edge, about 1 cm (½ in) apart, careful not to cut all the way through the pastry. Cut a small hole in the centre to allow steam to escape.
8. Carefully transfer the pie, on its baking paper, to the hot baking tray and cook for 10 minutes at 200°C fan (400°F) and then reduce the oven temperature to 180°C fan (350°F) and cook for a further 25–30 minutes, until it's as beautifully deep golden as possible (but not burnt!).
9. Once cooked, leave to cool on the tray for about 15 minutes before slicing into wedges and enjoying while warm.

Morel, leek and tarragon pie

SERVES 4

DIFFICULTY 🍄🍄

FILLING

1 tbsp vegetable oil
15 g (½ oz) butter
250 g (9 oz) waxy potatoes, quartered
150 g (5 oz) button mushrooms, halved
100 g (3½ oz) morel mushrooms (or other wild mushrooms), halved
1 medium leek
2 tbsps plain (all-purpose) flour
100 ml (3½ fl oz) dry vermouth (or white wine)
200 ml (7 fl oz) (good-quality) vegetable stock
small bunch of tarragon, leaves picked and chopped
sea salt flakes and ground black pepper
100 ml (3½ fl oz) double (heavy) cream

PASTRY

100 g (3 ½ oz) self-raising (self-rising) flour
¼ tsp fine salt
50 g (2 oz) vegetable suet
4–5 tbsps water
1 egg, beaten

TO SERVE

tenderstem broccoli or green beans

Morels give this pie filling an earthy and hearty flavour, while the tarragon gives it a herbal complexity. If you've not cooked with tarragon before, this is a beautiful way to introduce it into your kitchen, as the flavour combination is really bold. Mushroom and anise are a great pair and they also have a shared love of cream, which is what marries this dish together in the final step.

1. Preheat the oven to 160°C fan (320°F).
2. Make the filling by adding the vegetable oil and butter to a frying pan (skillet) over a high heat. Add the potatoes and fry for 5 minutes until they are lightly golden at the edges. Transfer to a bowl, but leave the butter and oil behind in the pan. Add the mushrooms and leek to the pan and cook for another 5 minutes, to soften. Once the mushrooms have produced a little liquid, add in the flour and stir to cook well for 2 minutes then pour in the vermouth and stir to get rid of any lumps. Add in the stock, stir well and bring to the boil then remove from the heat.
3. Pour the mushroom mixture over the potatoes and finally add in the chopped tarragon and season generously with salt and pepper and stir to mix. Transfer to a 2-litre (2-quart) pie dish and leave to cool slightly while you make the pastry.
4. Stir the flour, salt and suet together in a large bowl. Add in the water and use a wooden spoon to stir until it has just come together then roll out to the same shape as your pie dish. Place the pastry on top of the pie filling and crimp the edges to seal. Cut a circle in the centre, about 4 cm (1½ in) wide, but leave the cut pastry circle in there. Brush with egg all over.
5. Bake for 1 hour until golden on top then remove from the oven and carefully remove the circle in the centre. Pour in the double cream straight away and then replace the pastry circle and leave the pie to sit for 5–10 minutes.
6. Serve warm, with some greens on the side.

Mushroom stroganoff

SERVES 4

DIFFICULTY 🍄

15 g (½ oz) butter
1 tbsp olive oil
1 onion, finely sliced
2 garlic cloves, sliced
500 g (1 lb 2 oz) mixed wild mushrooms, cut into bitesize pieces
100 ml (3½ fl oz) brandy
1 tsp hot paprika
1 tsp tomato purée (paste)
1 tbsp plain (all-purpose) flour
400 ml (13 fl oz) vegetable stock
1 tbsp English mustard
2 tsps vegan Worcestershire sauce
150 ml (5 fl oz) sour cream
sea salt flakes and freshly ground black pepper

TO SERVE

chopped gherkins, essential
chopped parsley
cooked rice (I like fluffy basmati) or crusty bread
squeeze of lemon, optional

Alongside the Vol-au-vents on page 26, I'd like to include this other slightly retro dish. It's likely it originated from Eastern Europe or Russia. So, I'd like to cheekily suggest serving this with an ice-cold vodka. Typically made with beef, but mushrooms are a key element – I think a mixture of wild mushrooms work fantastically as the stars of the show.

1. Heat the butter and olive oil in a large sauté pan or deep frying pan (skillet) over a medium–high heat. Cook the onion in the butter and oil for 5–7 minutes until softened and beginning to caramelize.
2. Add in the garlic and mushrooms and cook for a further 7–9 minutes until their liquid has evaporated and they have also begun to caramelize. At which point, pour in the brandy to deglaze the pan, scraping off any caramelization on the bottom, and bring to a boil until the liquid has evaporated completely (1–2 minutes).
3. Stir through the paprika, tomato purée and flour and cook for 2 minutes, stirring constantly until the aroma of paprika is in the air.
4. Pour in the stock, a little at a time, mixing well, to avoid any lumps of flour. Once you have added all the stock, stir through the mustard and Worcestershire sauce, and season with salt and pepper. Bring to a gentle simmer for 10 minutes.
5. Finally, stir through the sour cream and gently heat through until hot, but do not boil.
6. Serve straight away topped with gherkins and parsley, with a side of rice or bread and a squeeze of lemon, if your sour cream isn't too sharp.

Seasonal greens and roasted wild mushroom risotto

SERVES 4

DIFFICULTY

100 g (3½ oz) large-leaf spinach (or kale/cavolo nero)
1 garlic clove
1 tbsp lemon juice
80 g (3 oz) butter
1 onion, finely chopped
300 g (10½ oz) risotto rice
150 ml (5 fl oz) white wine
1 litre (34 fl oz) vegetable stock, hot
100 g (3½ oz) morel mushrooms, halved
2 tsps olive oil
80 g (3 oz) pecorino, finely grated
sea salt flakes and freshly ground black pepper

TO SERVE
mascarpone

Risotto and mushrooms often go hand in hand. Morel mushrooms are one of the biggest treats in their short season from April to June. Some mushroom lovers see them as a sign of spring. You can top this risotto with any kind of wild mushrooms, perhaps whichever are in season, and match them with the appropriate greens - spinach matched with morels or cavolo nero paired with chanterelle. What grows together, goes together.

1. Preheat the oven to 180°C fan (350°F), or if you'd prefer to do it all on the hob, skip this step.
2. Bring a large pan of water to the simmer and boil the spinach (or kale) and garlic for 1–2 minutes. Drain and transfer to a high-powered food processor along with the lemon juice and two-thirds of the butter. Blend until completely smooth.
3. Heat the remaining butter in a sauté pan over a medium heat and cook the onion for 4–5 minutes until softened but not browned. Add in the rice and cook for 1 minute, stirring to toast, and then pour in the white wine and cook for 1–2 minutes until it has bubbled away.
4. Add a third of the stock and reduce the heat to medium-low. Cook for 20 minutes, stirring often, adding in the rest of the stock a little at a time once the first third has been absorbed by the rice (you may not need all the stock, it will depend how hot your pan is).
5. Meanwhile place the mushrooms on a baking tray, season with salt and pepper and drizzle with olive oil and cook in the oven for 10–12 minutes (or pan fry for 6–8 minutes).
6. Stir the blended green sauce and the pecorino through the rice and season with salt and pepper. Warm through for 30 seconds then remove from the heat.
7. Serve topped with a dollop of mascarpone, the morel mushrooms and a crack of fresh black pepper.

Portobello mushroom moussaka

SERVES 6

DIFFICULTY

BÉCHAMEL

75 g (2½ oz) butter
75 g (2½ oz) plain (all-purpose) flour
750 ml (25 fl oz) whole milk
grating of whole nutmeg
2 egg yolks

MUSHROOM RAGU

1 tbsp extra virgin olive oil
1 onion, finely diced
250 g (9 oz) portobello mushrooms, finely chopped
1 garlic clove, chopped
60 ml (2 fl oz) red wine
250 g (9 oz) pre-cooked beluga or puy lentils
1 x 400 g (14 oz) tin chopped tomatoes
2 tsps dried oregano
1 cinnamon stick
1 bay leaf
150 ml (5 fl oz) water
sea salt flakes and freshly ground black pepper

ASSEMBLY

2 tbsps extra virgin olive oil
2 aubergine (eggplant), sliced in 1 cm (½ in) slices
300 g (10½ oz) waxy potatoes, peeled and sliced in ½ cm (¼ in) slices

Do not let the number of pots required to make this recipe put you off – this version of a classic Greek dish may very well end up being your new favourite thing to do with mushrooms.

1. Preheat the oven to 170°C fan (340°F).
2. Start by making the béchamel. Melt the butter in a saucepan over a medium-high heat then add the flour and cook through for 2–3 minutes, stirring constantly. Add the milk a little at the time, whisking between additions to get rid of any lumps. Once all the milk is added bring the béchamel briefly to the boil then remove from the heat. Season with salt, pepper and a grating of nutmeg. Once cooled slightly, whisk in the egg yolks.
3. For the mushroom ragu, heat the oil in a large frying pan (skillet) over a medium-high heat and fry the onion for 8–10 minutes until softened and beginning to turn golden. Add the mushrooms and cook for a further 8–10 minutes. Add the garlic in and cook for 1–2 minutes until the garlic is translucent then deglaze the pan with the red wine. Finally add in the lentils, chopped tomatoes, oregano, cinnamon, bay leaf and water and season with salt and pepper. Bring to a gentle simmer then reduce to low and cook for 15–20 minutes. Then remove the cinnamon and bay leaf.
4. For the aubergine, in a separate frying pan, heat 1 tablespoon of olive oil over a medium heat and add the sliced aubergine in a single layer (you will need to do this in batches). Season the top of the aubergine with salt and pepper and cook without moving for 5 minutes. Flip and then cook for a

further 5 minutes. Set aside and repeat with the rest of the aubergine.

5. For the potatoes, place the sliced potatoes in a small saucepan with a big pinch of salt and cover with cold water. Bring to the boil and once boiling, drain the potato and leave to steam in the colander/sieve over the hot pan.
6. To assemble, place the potatoes in a single layer at the bottom of a baking dish (approximately 20 x 30 cm/8 x 12 in), follow with the mushroom ragu in an even layer then a single layer of cooked aubergine and finally, spoon the béchamel over the top to cover everything.
7. Place into the oven for 35–40 minutes until the top is mottled golden. Leave to sit for 5–10 minutes before digging in.

Confit garlic mushroom mac and cheese

SERVES 4–6

DIFFICULTY

CONFIT GARLIC

1 whole garlic bulb
400 ml (13 fl oz) extra virgin olive oil
1 bay leaf
2 sprigs of rosemary (or thyme)

CHEESE SAUCE

1 onion, finely chopped
5 g (¼ oz) dried porcini, rehydrated in boiling water for 15 minutes and then drained
250 g (9 oz) chestnut mushrooms, sliced
2 tbsps plain (all-purpose) flour
500 ml (17 fl oz) whole milk
250 g (9 oz) Cheddar, grated
100 g (3½ oz) mozzarella, grated
50 g (2 oz) pecorino, grated
2 tsps (any) mustard
sea salt flakes and freshly ground black pepper

300 g (10½ oz) macaroni, cooked to instructions and drained
1 slice of stale sourdough bread, cut into small cubes

There is little in life more comforting than a warm cheesy bowl of pasta. This dish is best served with a sharp salad – some bitter leaves with the dressing from page 118 are my favourite. Keep the leftover confit garlic oil for any garlicy sautéing, dressings or drizzles.

1. Place the garlic bulb in your smallest saucepan and cover with just enough olive oil to submerge the garlic. Add in the bay leaf and rosemary. Place over a high heat for 3 minutes to warm up the oil and then turn down to the lowest heat possible and cook for about 25–35 minutes. Use tongs or a slotted spoon to remove the garlic from the oil and leave until cool enough to handle then squeeze the softened garlic cloves into a bowl and discard the skin and herbs. Reserve the oil.
2. Meanwhile, make the cheese sauce. Cook the chopped onion in 2 tablespoons of the garlic oil in a very large saucepan over a medium heat for 5–6 minutes until beginning to soften then stir in the porcini and half the chestnut mushrooms and cook for another 5–6 minutes until some of their moisture has evaporated and they have shrunk in size. Add the flour and cook for 1 minute further, while stirring. Pour a little of the milk in and stir vigorously to combine, repeat with a little of the milk at a time until you have added it all. Bring to a simmer then add two-thirds of the grated cheeses and mustard into the sauce along with the confit garlic cloves and stir. Once the cheese has melted, take the pan off the heat, stir in the cooked and drained pasta and season it all with salt and pepper.
3. Turn on the grill (broiler) to medium. Transfer the pasta and sauce to a large baking dish. Scatter the remaining mushrooms, cheese and bread cubes over the top and finally drizzle the whole thing with a little more confit garlic oil. Cook for 5–8 minutes until caramelized and golden on top and then serve warm with salad.

Buttermilk-fried mushroom burger with Big Mac sauce

SERVES 4

DIFFICULTY

BIG MAC SAUCE

125 g (4 oz) mayonnaise
1 tbsp yellow mustard
2 tbsps pickle/gherkin relish
1 tsp paprika
½ tsp onion powder
½ tsp garlic powder

BURGER

200 g (7 oz) hen of the woods (or oyster mushroom/enoki clusters)
50 g (2 oz) plain (all-purpose) flour
50 g (2 oz) cornflour (cornstarch)
1 tsp ground black pepper
½ tsp fine salt
100 ml (3½ fl oz) buttermilk
vegetable oil, for frying

TO SERVE

4 burger buns, toasted
1 tomato, sliced
½ iceberg lettuce, finely shredded
8 pickled gherkin slices

This juicy, crispy burger is a little indulgent but hits a craving bang on the mark. Best served with French fries. A bite-full of comfort with no drive-through required – nostalgic fast-food vibes with a satisfyingly meaty mushroom twist.

1. Mix all the Big Mac sauce ingredients together and set aside.
2. Pour the oil in a heavy-bottomed pan until about halfway up and heat until about 160°C (320°F).
3. Tear the hen of the woods mushrooms into burger-sized wedges.
4. Stir the flour, cornflour, pepper and salt together in a bowl. In a separate bowl, pour in the buttermilk.
5. Dip the mushroom wedges into the flour mix, then dip into the buttermilk to coat and back into the flour for another dusting.
6. Carefully lower the coated mushrooms into the oil and cook for 3–4 minutes until golden and crispy, flipping halfway through.
7. Remove from the oil and place on a cooling rack to drain the excess oil briefly.
8. Assemble the burger by spreading a little sauce on the bottom of all the buns, followed by tomato slices and a small handful of sliced lettuce, then place the warm fried mushrooms, a big dollop of Big Mac sauce and finally a couple of pickle slices. Place the lid of the bun on the burger and enjoy hot, with a side of fries if you like.

Mushroom, shallot and Stilton tart tatin

SERVES 3–4

DIFFICULTY

2 tsps extra virgin olive oil
8 shallots, halved
200 g (7 oz) chestnut mushrooms, sliced
3 tbsps caster (superfine) sugar
1 tbsp water
1 tbsp red wine vinegar
1 x 320 g (11 oz) sheet of puff pastry
50 g (2 oz) Stilton (or any other blue cheese)
sea salt flakes and freshly ground black pepper

Mushroom and blue cheese is one of my all-time favourite flavour combinations. The shallots and vinegary caramel come sweetly in to make what I can promise you will become a summertime lunch staple. Best served with a fresh salad or some sliced tomatoes and enjoyed with some close friends and a glass of chilled white wine!

1. Preheat the oven to 180°C fan (350°F).
2. Start by heating half the olive oil in a 25 cm (10 in) ovenproof non-stick frying pan (skillet). Add in the halved shallots and cook for 5 minutes over a medium-high heat, turning halfway through. Then remove the shallots and set them aside on a plate.
3. Add the remaining olive oil to the pan and cook the sliced mushrooms for 3 minutes, turning halfway then turn them out onto a plate.
4. Wipe the pan clean with paper towel then add in the sugar and water and shake the pan to stir (do not stir with a spoon). Heat for 4–5 minutes, shaking often, until the sugar has turned golden and smells like caramel. Remove the pan from the heat and quickly (and carefully!) add in the vinegar. Shake to mix, but careful as this may spit slightly.
5. Add the cooked shallots into the centre of the pan, cut side down and layer the sliced mushrooms, overlapping in a ring around the edge. Season all over with salt and pepper.
6. Cut the pastry to a circle just larger than the pan (keep any offcuts in the freezer for another recipe, such as Vol-au-vents, page 26). Lay the pastry over the mushrooms and shallots, tucking the edges in. Use a knife to score a hole in the centre of the pastry, to allow steam to escape.
7. Cook in the oven for 20 minutes then carefully flip out onto a baking tray, scatter the blue cheese over the shallots and return to the oven, filling side up, for a further 5 minutes.
8. Cut into slices and enjoy warm.

Creamy mushroom and garlic bucatini

SERVES 4

DIFFICULTY 🍄

500 g (1 lb 2 oz) bucatini (or spaghetti)
2 tbsps olive oil
400 g (14 oz) shimeji mushrooms
4 garlic cloves, sliced
60 ml (2 fl oz) white wine
150 g (5 oz) crème fraîche
150 ml (5 fl oz) double (heavy) cream
60 g (2 oz) pecorino, grated, plus extra to serve
4 tbsps (vegetarian) pesto, optional
sea salt flakes and freshly ground black pepper

When I think of cooking with mushrooms, this is the first dish that comes to mind. Particularly for trying to get kids to really enjoy mushrooms. Creamy mushroom pasta is always rich and satisfying and the shimeji mushrooms are particularly good at wrapping themselves round the bucatini, which is a round spaghetti-esque pasta shape with a hollow middle.

1. Cook the pasta in a large pan of salted water until al dente, then drain but reserve about 200 ml (7 fl oz) of pasta water.
2. Meanwhile, brown the mushrooms in olive oil in your largest frying pan (skillet) over a high heat for 4–5 minutes.
3. Add in the garlic and cook for 1–2 minutes until fragrant then quickly add in the white wine, to deglaze the pan. Once the wine has evaporated, stir the crème fraîche, cream and cheese through the mushrooms and cook through for 1 minute.
4. Add the drained pasta to the mushrooms along with the pesto, if using, and the reserved pasta water and season with salt and pepper. Bubble away over a high heat for 1–2 minutes, stirring constantly until the sauce has thickened and has coated the pasta completely.
5. Serve up, topped with extra black pepper and grated cheese, if you like, and enjoy hot.

Bistro button mushroom salad

with a shallot and mustard dressing

SERVES 2 AS A MAIN OR 4 AS A SIDE

DIFFICULTY

SALAD

200 g (7 oz) waxy potatoes
100 g (3½ oz) green beans
75 g (2½ oz) button mushrooms, very finely sliced
50 g (2 oz) radishes, sliced
150 g (5 oz) salad leaves (such as frisée or butter lettuce)
50 g (2 oz) chicory (endive, or other bitter leaf), chopped
125 g (4 oz) goat's cheese or Stilton crumbled/cubed
50 g (2 oz) toasted walnuts, chopped
5 g mixture of fresh herbs (parsley, chives, tarragon and chervil), chopped

SHALLOT DRESSING

2 shallots, finely sliced
1½ tbsps sherry vinegar
4 tbsps extra virgin olive oil
1 tbsp honey
1½ tsps Dijon mustard
sea salt flakes and freshly ground black pepper

There are quite a few things that French bistros do better than anywhere else, and hearty fresh enormous salads are one of them. This mushroom salad is a nod to a bistro. Serve as a main dish or as a side. You can make this with any cheese you fancy and also throw in some extra ingredients such as olives or croutons, if you like.

1. Place the potatoes in a saucepan, cover with cold water and season well. Bring to the boil and cook for 10–15 minutes until just tender. Drain and leave to cool. Once cool, slice roughly.
2. Blanch the green beans in boiling water for 3 minutes, then drain and plunge into iced water to cool quickly. Drain again and chop.
3. Make the dressing by placing the shallots in a jam jar (Mason jar). Add the vinegar and some salt and stir. Leave to sit for at least 5 minutes, but as long as you like. Add the remaining dressing ingredients and place the lid on the jar and shake vigorously to emulsify.
4. Add all the salad ingredients to a large mixing bowl, keeping aside half the herbs for garnish. Add in half the dressing and toss to coat all the ingredients.
5. Divide the salad evenly into serving bowls, drizzle the remaining dressing over the top and finish with the reserved herbs.

Pan-fried gnocchi with squash and crispy sage

SERVES 4

DIFFICULTY 🍄🍄

SQUASH PURÉE

1 x small butternut squash (about 700 g/1 lb 9 oz), halved
2 garlic cloves, peel on
2 shallots, halved
1 tbsp extra virgin olive oil
½ tsp chilli flakes
80 ml (3 fl oz) double (heavy) cream
sea salt flakes and freshly ground black pepper

GNOCCHI

1 tbsp olive oil
20 sage leaves
100 g (3½ oz) chestnut mushrooms, sliced
50 g (2 oz) butter
500 g (1 lb 2 oz) gnocchi

grated pecorino, to serve

There's something undeniably comforting about gnocchi – maybe it's the texture of the little dough cushions, their soft golden edges and how they are so deliciously chewy. This bowl with creamy squash at the bottom and topped with crispy sage on top is a perfect invitation to dig in and enjoy.

1. Preheat the oven to 180°C fan (350°F).
2. Scoop out the seeds of the squash and discard them. Place the halved squash on a baking tray, cut side up and place the garlic cloves and shallots in the void you have just removed the seeds from. Drizzle all over with olive oil, season with salt and scatter over the chilli flakes. Bake in the oven for 50–55 minutes, until the squash is soft.
3. Once cooked, remove the peel from the cooked garlic and add the cloves to a food processor along with the shallot and the flesh of the squash, discarding the skin. Pour in the cream and blend until smooth.
4. Transfer to a pan to keep warm over a low heat to serve.
5. Heat the olive oil in a large frying pan (skillet). Once hot, fry the sage leaves for 10 seconds until crispy but not burnt. Remove from the oil with tongs and transfer them to a piece of paper towel.

(Continued overleaf)

Then add the sliced mushrooms into the pan and fry for 2–3 minutes until golden, transfer to a plate to set aside. Turn down to low and add the butter to the pan and leave to melt.

6. Meanwhile, bring a large pan of salted water to the boil and add the gnocchi. Cook to packet instructions then drain completely and add into the pan with butter in. Increase the heat to high and cook for 1–2 minutes to get golden crispy edges.
7. Serve the puree on the base of the plate, topped with the fried gnocchi, mushrooms, crispy sage and finally some grated cheese.

Mushroom and blue cheese fusilli with pangrattato

SERVES 4

DIFFICULTY

2 tbsps olive oil
80 g (3 oz) sourdough breadcrumbs
¼ tsp chilli flakes
zest of ½ lemon
toasted walnuts, chopped
150 g (5 oz) mushrooms (chestnut, button or wild), sliced
150 g (5 oz) radicchio (or chicory/endive), sliced
150 g (5 oz) tenderstem broccoli, sliced
500 g (1 lb 2 oz) fusilli (or another small pasta shape such as orecchiette)
250 g (9 oz) Dolcelatte
100 g (3½ oz) crème fraîche
sea salt flakes and freshly ground black pepper

TO SERVE
grated pecorino
4 fried eggs, optional

This is a dish that my brother, a mushroom enthusiast who rarely steps foot in front of the kitchen counter, has cooked for me. If he can make it as delicious as he does, I decided it would be a brilliant, easy dish to include, in the spirit of encouraging even the cooks with the most basic skills to cook with mushrooms. The flavours are so mouth-watering, and it's about as umami as a dish gets, with blue cheese, mushrooms, walnuts and egg. Asking my brother what vegetable he usually stirs through this sauce – Broccoli? Chard? – was met with, 'What do you mean? I consider the mushrooms one of my 5 a week!'

1. Make the pangrattato by adding half the olive oil to a frying pan (skillet) and fry the breadcrumbs over a high heat for 3–4 minutes until crispy. Stir the chilli flakes, lemon zest and walnuts through and season with salt. Tip into a bowl and set aside.
2. Wipe the frying pan clean and add the rest of the oil and the mushrooms. Sauté for 5–6 minutes over a medium heat. Add in the radicchio and broccoli for 2–3 minutes more.
3. Meanwhile, cook the pasta in a large pan of boiling salted water, according to packet instructions.
4. Stir the blue cheese into the mushrooms until melted and follow with the crème fraîche. Warm through and then stir the pasta into the mushrooms. Season well with salt and pepper.
5. Serve the pasta in bowls and top with the pangrattato, pecorino and a fried egg, if you like.

Blue cheese fonduta

with roasted mushrooms, beetroot and croutons

SERVES 4 - 6

DIFFICULTY

600 g (1 lb 5 oz) beetroot (beet), peeled
1 red onion, cut into wedges
4 tbsps olive oil
200 g (7 oz) chestnut mushrooms, sliced
2 sprigs of rosemary
1 tbsp honey
200 g (7 oz) sourdough, cut into 2.5 cm (1 in) cubes
200g (7 oz) Stilton (or Dolcelatte)
100 g (3½ oz) crème fraîche
sea salt flakes and freshly ground black pepper

A total mix of textures come together to make this dish what it is. The earthy flavours of mushrooms and beetroot work deliciously with a silky creamy blue cheese sauce. Could be served as a sharing plate or as individual starters.

1. Preheat the oven to 200°C fan (400°F).
2. Peel and cut the beetroot into 2.5 cm (1 in) wedges. Put in your largest roasting tray along with the onion, olive oil, salt and pepper and roast for 20 minutes. Add the mushrooms and rosemary and toss with the beetroot then drizzle with honey. Cook for 20 minutes and then add in the cubed sourdough and toss it through the vegetables. Return to the oven for a further 10 minutes.
3. Once the vegetables are almost cooked, make the fonduta. Warm the Stilton over a gentle heat in a saucepan and once melted remove from the heat, add in the crème fraîche and stir to combine.
4. Spread the fonduta over a large shallow bowl, top with the cooked vegetables and croutons and eat while warm.

SOME-THING ON THE SIDE

When they are not taking centre stage as the main course, mushrooms can be a killer accompaniment to vegetable and meat dishes alike. They may be on the side, but they will not go unnoticed.

Smacked cucumber and wood ear mushroom salad

SERVES 4

DIFFICULTY

15 g (½ oz) dried wood ear mushrooms
1 whole cucumber
small bunch of coriander (cilantro), chopped
1 spring onion (scallion), sliced, to serve

DRESSING

2 tsps crispy chilli oil
2 tsps Chinese black vinegar (or rice vinegar)
½ tsp caster (superfine) sugar
1 tbsp soy sauce
2 tsps light sesame seeds
1 tsp sesame oil
1 small garlic clove, crushed
¼ tsp Sichuan peppercorns, crushed, optional

This is a Chinese cuisine classic. If you want to make it in advance, keep the cucumber separate from the seasonings until the last minute and then stir all together to serve. The addition of the Sichuan peppercorns make for a spicier dish, if that's your preference.

1. Pour boiling water over the dried mushrooms and leave to rehydrate for at least 30 minutes (or overnight).
2. In a large bowl, make a dressing by stirring together the chilli oil, vinegar, sugar, soy sauce, sesame seeds and oil, garlic and peppercorns, if using, until the sugar has dissolved.
3. Next, cut the cucumber in half lengthways, use a teaspoon to remove the seeds and discard them. Turn the cucumber halves skin side up on the chopping board and then bash them with a rolling pin before cutting them into roughly 2 cm (¾ in) pieces.
4. Drain and finely slice the mushrooms and add to the dressing along with the chopped cucumber and coriander, and stir to combine.
5. Top with spring onion to serve and enjoy straight away.

Sticky shiitake and shimeji rice

SERVES 4

DIFFICULTY 🍄🍄

300 g (10½ oz) glutinous rice
1 tbsp vegetable oil
200 g (7 oz) mixture of shiitake and shimeji mushrooms, sliced
4 round shallots (or 2 banana shallots), finely chopped
2 cm (¾ in) fresh ginger root, finely chopped
1 garlic clove, crushed
2 tbsps mirin
3 tbsps soy sauce
2 tsps caster (superfine) sugar
spring onions (scallions), sliced, to serve

This gently flavoured rice side dish is a perfect, delicate, chewy accompaniment to a meal. The trick is to cook it on the lowest heat possible. If your hob is a little fierce, you may need to add a touch more water.

1. Wash the rice a few times until the water runs clear then tip it into a bowl and cover with water. Leave to soak for at least 1 hour, or overnight.
2. Heat the oil in a frying pan (skillet) over a high heat and fry the mushrooms for 2–3 minutes before adding the shallots, ginger and garlic and frying for a further minute. Take the pan off the heat and add in the mirin, soy sauce and sugar.
3. Drain the rice from its soaking water and add to a saucepan with a snug-fitting lid. Pour in 360 ml (12 fl oz) of water and spoon the mushroom mix on top of the rice in an even layer. Bring the rice to a boil over a high heat and, as soon as it begins to boil, place the lid on the pan and turn the heat down to the lowest setting possible.
4. Cook on low for 15 minutes and then turn the heat off but leave the lid on the pan for a further 10 minutes.
5. Enjoy hot, topped with sliced spring onions.

Porcini and potato gratin

SERVES 4

DIFFICULTY

5 g (¼ oz) dried porcini
1 tbsp extra virgin olive oil, plus extra for drizzling
1 onion, finely sliced
200 ml (7 fl oz) double (heavy) cream
60 ml (2 fl oz) vegetable stock
600 g (1 lb 2 oz) Maris Piper potatoes, peeled and thinly sliced
125 g (4 oz) fresh porcini (or chestnut) mushrooms, finely sliced
sea salt flakes and freshly ground black pepper

If you can find fresh porcini, then you are very lucky and you can use them. If not – substitute in fresh chestnut mushrooms (as well as the dried porcini). The trick here is to slice all the ingredients as thinly as possible – use a mandolin if you have one.

1. Preheat the oven to 170°C fan (340°F).
2. Place the dried porcini in a heatproof bowl and cover with boiling water. Leave to sit for 5–10 minutes.
3. Heat the oil in a frying pan (skillet) over a medium heat and fry the onions for 8–10 minutes until softened and beginning to brown. Remove from the heat and stir through the cream, stock, sliced potatoes and mushrooms and season well with salt and pepper.
4. Drain the dried porcini, chop finely and add into the potato mix.
5. Layer the potato mix in a shallow baking dish (about 15 x 20 cm/6 x 8 in).
6. Drizzle the top with a little more olive oil and then place into the oven for 40 minutes.

Mushroom and peppercorn sauce

SERVES 4

DIFFICULTY 🍄

15 g (½ oz) butter
1 tbsp extra virgin olive oil
1 shallot, finely chopped
200 g (7 oz) chestnut or button mushrooms, finely sliced
1 garlic clove, crushed
2 tbsps green peppercorns in brine, drained
150 ml (5 fl oz) Madeira (or fino sherry)
200 ml (7 fl oz) double (heavy) cream
sea salt flakes and freshly ground black pepper

This sauce is a flavour explosion – the rich tastes of green peppercorns and Madeira work like an umami dream alongside the mushrooms. It pairs deliciously with steak, pies and even potatoes.

1. Heat the butter and oil in a frying pan (skillet) over a medium heat and cook the shallot for 5–6 minutes until softened but not browned.
2. Add the mushrooms and cook for 10–12 minutes until they have shrunk to half their size and the moisture has all evaporated, adding the garlic for the final 2 minutes.
3. Pour in the green peppercorns and Madeira and bubble away for 1–2 minutes to deglaze the pan.
4. Finally, turn the heat down to low, stir in the cream and season to taste with salt and pepper. Heat through for 2–3 minutes, lightly simmering.
5. Serve warm.

Mushroom egg fried rice

SERVES 4 AS A SIDE OR 2 AS A MAIN

DIFFICULTY

3 eggs
250 g (9 oz) leftover cooked rice (or 125 g/ 4 oz rice, cooked and cooled)
2 tbsps vegetable (or groundnut) oil
2 spring onions (scallions), chopped
1 carrot, peeled and finely chopped
50 g (2 oz) shiitake, oyster or chestnut mushrooms, finely diced
50 g (2 oz) sweetheart/ hispi cabbage, finely chopped
1 tbsp soy sauce
1 tsp sesame oil
1 tsp rice vinegar
½ tsp sugar
pinch of sea salt flakes
chilli oil, to drizzle

The best thing to do with leftover rice is make it into a new dish the next day and egg fried rice is just my favourite way to do that! I like this best made from sushi or short grain rice but you can use anything you have, from basmati to jasmine. It's a great way to use up other leftovers too, such as cooked vegetables or meats. Just chop them finely and add them in. Ideally, have everything chopped to the same kind of size, for a perfect egg fried rice texture. If you are cooking rice for onigiri (page 54) or something else, you can plan ahead and cook extra to make a delicious fried rice lunch the next day.

1. Prepare all the ingredients and line them up next to the hob along with a large empty bowl for the cooked rice.
2. Crack the eggs into another large bowl, season with a pinch of salt and beat with a fork. Stir the cooked, cold rice into the beaten egg until there are no clumps of rice.
3. Place a wok (or large sauté pan) over a high heat and heat for a couple of minutes until very hot. Add in 1 tablespoon of the oil and once hot, add in the eggy rice. Fry for 2–3 minutes, stirring constantly, then remove the rice from the pan into the prepared bowl.
4. Add the remaining 1 tablespoon of oil into the pan along with the spring onions, carrot, mushrooms and cabbage. Fry for 2–3 minutes, stirring constantly until fragrant. Add the rice back into the wok, along with the soy sauce, sesame oil, rice vinegar and sugar and stir fry for 1 minute more.
5. Serve hot, topped with a drizzle of chilli oil.

Ginger stir-fried mushrooms and pak choi

SERVES 4

DIFFICULTY

1 tsp vegetable oil
200 g (7 oz) button, chestnut or shiitake mushrooms, sliced
2.5cm (1 in) fresh root ginger, roughly chopped
2 spring onions (scallions), chopped
2–4 dried chillies (or ¼ tsp dried chilli flakes)
8 baby or 4 large pak choi, halved or quartered
2 tbsps water

SAUCE

1 tbsp cornflour (cornstarch)
2 tbsps water
2 tbsps mushroom stir-fry sauce (vegetarian oyster sauce)
1 tbsp soy sauce
1 tsp Shaoxing wine or mirin

A very quick to throw together side dish that complements many a meal. Great served alongside rice or noodles. It uses mushroom stir-fry sauce – the store-bought vegetarian version of oyster sauce, which takes its rich savouriness from mushrooms. The ginger brightens it all up and makes this an equally refreshing and wholesome plate.

1. First, mix the sauce ingredients together in a bowl and set aside.
2. For the stir-fry, heat the vegetable oil in a lidded frying pan (skillet) over a medium-high heat and fry the mushrooms for 3–4 minutes before adding the ginger, spring onions and chillies for 1 minute.
3. Next, wash the pak choi, but do not shake off the excess water, and add into the mushroom mix. Stir, and place the lid on the pan for 3–4 minutes.
4. Remove the lid and add in the sauce, stirring constantly to cook for 1–2 minutes until thickened and darkened slightly.
5. Remove from the heat and serve hot.

TREATS TO COMPLETE

Mushrooms in desserts?! Hear me out. These all utilize mushroom coffee and lion's mane powder – a superfood that nourishes both body and mind. These may be the kind of recipes you might not expect in a mushroom book but will probably want to make again and again.

Lion's mane hot chocolate

SERVES 2

DIFFICULTY 🍄

400 ml (13 fl oz) milk (dairy or oat)
40 g (1½ oz) milk chocolate, chopped
40 g (1½ oz) dark chocolate, chopped
2 tsps lion's mane powder
40 ml (1½ fl oz) double (heavy) cream (or oat cream), lightly whipped
2 tbsps vegan marshmallows
cocoa powder or grated chocolate, to dust

A brain-boosting sweet treat. Lion's mane powder really adds to the creaminess of this hot chocolate especially when it's made with oat milk. Perfect for a cosy bit of mindful indulgence. Comfort, with benefits.

1. Heat the milk in a pan or in an electric milk-frother. Once hot, add in both chocolates and the lion's mane powder and set on a gentle heat to melt and combine.
2. Pour into mugs and top with a dollop of whipped cream, a scattering of marshmallows and a dusting of cocoa powder or grated chocolate.

Dirty mushroom martini

SERVES 4

DIFFICULTY

4 small or 1 large dried shiitake mushroom
1 dried porcini mushroom
4 tbsps water
1 tsp caster (superfine) sugar
2 tsps lime juice (or white wine vinegar)
½ tsp sea salt
175 ml (6 fl oz) gin or vodka
120 ml (4 fl oz) dry vermouth
ice

A twist on a classic dirty martini by using mushroom pickling liquid instead of olive brine. Temperature is everything here, so ensure that your cocktails are served ice cold – keep your alcohol in the fridge and, if you have space, chill your glasses in the freezer. In the words of a great martini drinking friend of mine, 'It should take three sips to drink – a warm martini is a wasted martini'.

1. Place the dried mushrooms in a heatproof jar or jug.
2. Bring the water, sugar, lime juice and salt to a boil in a small pan and immediately pour the pickling liquor over the mushrooms. Leave to pickle (and cool) for at least 1 hour, or overnight.
3. Remove the porcini mushroom and discard.
4. Chill four martini glasses either by putting them in the freezer for a few minutes or by filling with ice and water and leaving them to sit while you prepare the cocktail.
5. In a jug or large glass, pour the gin or vodka, vermouth and as much of the mushroom pickling liquid as you like (or all!). Add a handful of ice and stir for 2–3 minutes, until the outside of the glass feels ice cold.
6. Pour away the iced water in the glasses and add one pickled shiitake into each glass (or one-quarter of the mushroom if you used a large one).
7. Pour the chilled martini into the glasses through a small sieve or cocktail strainer, and serve immediately.

Lion's mane iced coconut latte

SERVES 1

DIFFICULTY

2 tsps mushroom-blend coffee powder (or 1 tsp of lion's mane powder and 1 shot of espresso)
70 ml (1 fl oz) boiling water
1 tsp maple syrup
½ tsp vanilla bean paste
ice
100 ml (3½ fl oz) coconut milk drink (or evaporated coconut milk)

Lion's mane powder is a fascinating superfood, prized for its potential to support focus, clarity and memory. Adding it into your daily coffee is a great way to boost your mental capacity.

1. Place the mushroom-blend coffee powder in a heatproof jug and add the freshly boiled water. Stir in the maple syrup and vanilla bean paste until dissolved and leave to cool. (If using lion's mane powder, stir this into the hot espresso with the maple syrup and vanilla bean paste and omit the boiling water).
2. Fill your serving glass with ice and pour in the coconut milk.
3. Once the coffee has cooled, give it another stir to make sure there is no sediment at the bottom and then pour it over the coconut milk.
4. Enjoy your beautiful mushroom ice-cold boost, daily.

White chocolate, mushroom matcha and macadamia cookies

MAKES 12 COOKIES

DIFFICULTY

3 tsps matcha mushroom powder, plus extra for dusting
1½ tsps boiling water
150 g (5 oz) butter, softened
75 g (2½ oz) caster (superfine) sugar
75 g (2½ oz) soft light brown sugar
1 egg, beaten
250 g (9 oz) plain (all-purpose) flour
pinch of salt
½ tsp bicarbonate of soda (baking soda)
100 g (3½ oz) white chocolate, broken into pieces
50 g (2 oz) macadamia nuts

You can keep these unbaked in your refrigerator for a week or in the freezer for 3 months - just add 2 minutes to the baking time if cooking from frozen. I like to do this so I can take one out at a time and whack it in the oven it when I fancy a freshly baked cookie. What a treat!

1. Preheat the oven to 170°C fan (340°F) and line two baking trays (pans) with baking parchment.
2. Start by dissolving the matcha mushroom powder in a small bowl with the boiling water. Leave to cool slightly.
3. Use a wooden spoon to cream together the butter and sugars until there are no lumps, and you have a paste. Stir in the matcha mix and the egg until all combined.
4. In a separate bowl, combine the flour, salt and bicarbonate of soda. Once mixed, stir this into the wet matcha mixture until just fully combined. Add the white chocolate and nuts and stir everything together to form the cookie dough.
5. Divide the dough into 12 balls, then press each one down to flatten slightly. Sprinkle with a little more matcha powder, if you like.
6. Place six cookie balls on each tray and bake for 10–12 minutes (remember that cookies harden a lot as they cool but should still be soft in the middle).
7. Leave to cool slightly on the tray and then enjoy warm or once cool.

Mushroom coffee tiramisu

SERVES 4–6

DIFFICULTY

- 4 tsps mushroom-blend coffee powder
- 400 ml (13 fl oz) boiling water
- 1 tbsp coffee liqueur, optional
- 2 egg yolks
- 75 g (2½ oz) soft light brown sugar
- 2 tbsps Marsala (or Madeira)
- 250 g (9 oz) mascarpone
- 250 ml (8½ fl oz) double (heavy) cream
- 2 tsps vanilla bean paste
- 24 sponge fingers (ladyfingers/savoiardi)
- 1 tbsp cocoa powder
- ¼ tsp mushroom powder, optional

This recipe is easy to double up if you're serving a dinner party of people. A tiramisu is probably one of the world's most-loved desserts and this mushroom coffee version is no exception. Best enjoyed with a glass of chilled dessert wine after an evening of over-indulgence.

1. Start by making the coffee. Mix the mushroom coffee powder with the boiling water and coffee liquor, if using, and then pour into a deep tray or shallow bowl and place in the refrigerator to cool.
2. Next, whisk the egg yolks, sugar and Marsala together in a large heatproof bowl and place it over a pan of lightly simmering water (without the bowl touching the water). Continue to whisk the mixture for 4–6 minutes until doubled in size and lightened in colour. Place in the refrigerator for at least 10 minutes, to cool slightly.
3. In a bowl, combine the mascarpone, cream and vanilla bean paste.
4. Remove the egg yolk mixture from the fridge and add in one-third of the cream and mascarpone mix, and whisk to incorporate. Add the rest in two more additions, whisking well between each one, until there are no lumps, and you have a smooth creamy mix.
5. Next, take the coffee out of the fridge and dunk 12 of the sponge fingers into the cooled coffee mixture, one at a time, for 1 second on each side, placing each one uniformly in a single layer on the bottom of a deep rectangular dish (about 20 x 30 cm/ 8 x 12 in). Top with half of the creamy mix and then repeat again with the remaining ingredients.
6. Leave in the fridge to set for at least 2 hours, or up for 24 hours. When ready to serve, stir together the cocoa powder and mushroom powder (if using) then remove the tiramisu from the fridge and dust with the cocoa mix to finish.
7. Use a spatula to portion out and serve cold.

Index

D

E

G

H

K

L

M

N

R

S

About the author

Evie Harbury is a food writer and a proud member of the Guild of Food Writers. After finishing her culinary training at Le Cordon Bleu, London, in 2016, Evie has since been working as a home economist, food stylist, recipe developer and chef. Originally from Bath, brought up between England and South Bohemia, Czech Republic, by an eccentric epicure of a father and an avant-garde, creative, baking mother, Evie is now an East London-based Bohemian (and has adopted some of these qualities).

Evie's writing work includes recipes for cookbooks, commercials and television series, as well as working on both film and stills as a food stylist and home economist. Her screen and print credits include several household names such as Mary Berry, Tom Kerridge, Giorgio Locatelli and Mary McCartney. These experiences have broadened her culinary knowledge and perspective. With a hunger for creating the most beautiful food, the most delicious plate, and the most satisfying creation in whatever form, she approaches every day in the kitchen as a bit of an adventure.

Shroom is Evie's second cookbook. Her first book, *My Bohemian Kitchen*, was published in 2025.

Acknowledgements

Thank you to my wonderful publisher, Heather, and the rest of the team at OH, Matt and James, for all your hard work and care in shaping this book. Isabel Atherton at Creative Authors – my fantastic agent who totally understands me – thanks for your belief, advice and calm guidance on my second book.

Thank you to my family – Mum, Dad, Dan, Sam and Sara – for eating more mushrooms in a concentrated period of time than you might usually be used to, while I was testing and developing these recipes. Thank you all for your unconditional support, your enthusiasm and your patience even after I've asked the same question about specific wild mushrooms for the third time. Are you SURE they tasted better deep-fried than pan-fried in butter?

Big thank you to Cristian, whose bold, bright photography brought these recipes to life. To Max, who has now prop-styled two out of two of my cookbooks with his beautiful, quirky finds. Let's try to keep those statistics up. To my brilliant food styling assistants for the shoot, Hattie and Katy, for both always having so much positive energy and keeping everything on track so brilliantly in the kitchen.

To my oldest friends, Tash and Dani, thank you for always cheering me on, even when I've been distracted, stressed or blabbering on about recipes, when you are trying to talk about something else entirely.

And finally, thanks to the late Richard Fortey, an old friend of my dad's, whose book *Close Encounters of the Fungal Kind* is fascinating and full of wonder. I wish I could tell him how much it inspired me through these pages.